A
Visitor's Guide
to
Hell

A
Visitor's Guide
to
Hell

A MANUAL *for* TEMPORARY

ENTRANTS *and* THOSE

WHO WOULD PREFER *to*

AVOID ETERNAL DAMNATION

Dr. Clint Archer

STERLING ETHOS
New York

STERLING ETHOS
New York

An Imprint of Sterling Publishing
387 Park Avenue South
New York, NY 10016

ISBN 978-1-4549-1365-8

Distributed in Canada by Sterling Publishing
℅ Canadian Manda Group, 165 Dufferin Street
Toronto, Ontario, Canada M6K 3H6
Distributed in the United Kingdom by GMC Distribution Services
Castle Place, 166 High Street, Lewes, East Sussex, England BN7 1XU
Distributed in Australia by Capricorn Link (Australia) Pty. Ltd.
P.O. Box 704, Windsor, NSW 2756, Australia

For information about custom editions, special sales, and premium and corporate purchases,
please contact Sterling Special Sales at 800-805-5489 or specialsales@sterlingpublishing.com.

Manufactured in the United States of America

2 4 6 8 10 9 7 5 3 1

www.sterlingpublishing.com

To Dr. John MacArthur and the faculty of
The Master's Seminary; their love for truth inspires
a generation and will echo in eternity.

✦ CONTENTS ✦

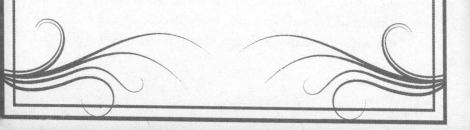

introduction

✦✦✦

Raising Hell

When I was a young boy, as an occasional treat we would spend the night at my cousins' home. Their house featured avant-garde interior design and some funky novelties—secret passageways, legless chairs hanging from chains, mirrored ceilings. These made every visit a fun exploration of alien territory. However, I avoided one place in the house: the Hell room. (I am not making any of this up.) The Hell room was a bathroom that had been painted entirely red: red walls, flooring, tiles, bath, toilet, towels—everything. And on the wall was a Styrofoam cutout of a cartoonish red devil complete with pitchfork. When the bath was drawn, billowing steam would fill the room, and my nightmares. No wonder my cousins hated bath time. It was Hell for them.

Many dismiss Hell as a mythological dimension used to scare children into compliance, not to be taken seriously as an adult. Devilish décor was all the rage in some avant-garde niches in the 1980s, much the way the paranormal TV genre is trending among teen viewers today. By surrounding ourselves with less-than-reverent depictions of a fiery afterlife, we've been desensitized to a bewildering Scriptural reality. We anesthetize the horrors of Hell by relegating the teachings of the Bible to the realm of academic debate or fanciful fiction. We put books about Hell and demons on the same shelf as novels about vampires and werewolves. But the difference between netherworld mythology and teachings about Hell is that the latter has been accepted as fact—not fiction—in every society and civilization in recorded history. This is what piques my curiosity about the subject to begin with. Most of us would consider it out of the ordinary if an adult insisted on the existence of Santa Claus or failed to grow out of his fear of the boogeyman, but the belief in Satan and Hell has been firmly held by billions of people of all ages over the centuries—people from all walks of life and possessing every level of education. This is intriguing. The Barna Research Group found in a poll that "an overwhelming majority of Americans continue to believe that there is life after death and that heaven and hell exist."

Let's face it: Hell is not a topic most people like to talk about, blog about, or teach their children about. The very word *Hell* is classified as a soap-in-the-mouth cussword in many homes. As kids we frustrated the tattletales by skirting the taboo word with a typographical code phrase: "Go to H. E. double hockey sticks!" Like sex and hemorrhoids, Hell is a topic unmentionable in polite company.

So why write a book about it? Why raise Hell?

⊹ THEOLOGIANS AND PROCTOLOGISTS ⊹

The reason to mention the unmentionable is simple: because a desire to avoid unpleasantness isn't a good enough reason to avoid thinking. We don't enjoy thinking about our digestive tracts, but we are all really glad there are textbooks on proctology. When we need to face the reality of trouble brewing in our nether regions, we know some expert has gallantly ventured into that course of study on our behalf. Rather than ignore the topic of Hell, we should embrace the information we have at our disposal, particularly teachings provided in the Bible— however disconcerting they may prove.

If Hell is not real, then it behooves us to explore why so many people in the world today and in centuries past believed in it. Why does humanity *need* Hell?

If, on the other hand, Hell is *real*, then ignoring it is not only futile but also foolish. It is unimaginably dangerous to sip the opiate of ignorance rather than face the proffered cure. Avoiding the subject in the hope that it is mere myth is the worst high-stakes gamble a person could ever make, akin to playing Russian roulette with one's eternal destiny.

✦ WE AGREE TO A DEGREE ✦

Almost every ancient religion in mankind's history has acknowledged the existence of a place or state of punishment for those who find themselves at odds with their religion's credo.

The consistency of this punitive concept is astonishing. This sounds like the start of a joke, but just imagine a Jewish rabbi, a Protestant pastor, a Catholic priest, a Muslim imam, a Hindu guru, and a Celtic druid agreeing on a single religious doctrine. Hell would be your best bet at finding common ground.

Religions tend to be mutually exclusive in their belief systems. Until postmodernism popularized relative thinking, everyone in history understood that not all religions could be correct. If souls spend eternity in an underworld like Hades, then they cannot also be annihilated, and simultaneously sent to a euphoric spirit realm, while being reincarnated as a rodent, and yet burning in Hell. Either they are *all* wrong, and there is an option no one has ever thought of, or *one* is right, and the rest are not.

✦ IN THE ABSENCE OF EYEWITNESSES ✦

So, given the fact that multiple religions do include some vision of an afterlife that resembles Hell but that there are also differing opinions about the specifics of how one gets there, how does one research this topic? Not to mention that it is quite frankly out of the realm of natural discovery. We would need an authoritative source, and although erudite opinions and claims at inside information abound, no one can prove that they have more credible knowledge about the afterlife than anyone else. Claims of firsthand experience cannot be proven, and they lack consensus. In other words, we all agree that, without someone we trust to have "been there, done that," we are all merely speculating on that which can never be known without supernatural revelation.

So, rather than survey the myriad potential sources of teachings about the afterlife, I will focus the attention of this book on the data found in the New Testament of the Bible, specifically the teachings of Jesus Christ. Much of the information about Hell in the New Testament will seem familiar to adherents of other religions—many intersections should be expected on this universally accepted religious theme. The teachings of Christ on Hell are a well-respected source because they are esteemed by Protestant and Catholic Christians, as well as Jews and Muslims. And although these major world religions would differ greatly on the place of Jesus in their respective worldviews, none dispute him as a trustworthy source of revelation about Hell. Muslims, Jews, and Christians all acknowledge Jesus as a prophet, possessing special insight and revelation about the afterlife, and many other faiths acknowledge his teachings as a source of ancient wisdom worth considering.

The description of Hell Jesus articulated is perfectly consistent with the views held by the Jews of his own day (remember that Jesus was a respected rabbi by his contemporary countrymen and is still viewed that way by many Jews). And of course, Christians of every stripe would consider the teachings of Jesus on Hell as the most authoritative available.

What many people don't know about the teachings of Jesus Christ is that, although he gave no picturesque descriptions of what Heaven is like, he did describe Hell graphically on several occasions.

It seems that Jesus showed no hesitation mentioning the unmentionable in polite company. And so, I hope you will extend to me the same leniency as I seek to relate to you the New Testament teachings on this—if you'll pardon the pun— very hot topic.

✦ MEMOIRS OF A DAMNED FOOL ✦

I have taken a liberty in this book that deserves explanation. Although there have been multiple books published purporting to be memoirs from a temporary journey to Hell, there is no evidence that anyone has ever gone to Hell and then come back to talk about it later. I detest the first-person narrative claims of self-styled Hell survivors. But, that said, there is an account in the New Testament where Jesus tells of a rich man who unexpectedly found himself damned to Hell by his own folly. The purpose of that story was for Jesus, the master storyteller, to make the somber doctrine of Hell come to life in vivid living color for his audience, so that they might appreciate the gravity and reality of Hell.

The brief sketch recorded in Luke 16:19–31 reads like a disturbing passage from a Stephen King novel, and if you will grant me some poetic license, I'd like to draw on the drama of that story and weave it into our guided tour of the afterlife. I'll do this by framing this teaching as a memoir written by the rich man in Jesus's story. My goal is to prevent us from discussing this bewildering subject in a merely abstract, theoretical way. Hell is about people, not statistics. Belief in the existence of such a horror is a personal matter with profound implications for the way we think, live, love, and worship.

✦ HITCHHIKER'S GUIDE TO HELL ✦

I love travel, and so I love guidebooks to help me prepare for what to expect. A good guidebook will supply a sense of the spirit of a place, its history, its climate, its demographics, and its culture. Reading a guidebook before a journey usually puts me in an adventurous frenzy. I salivate to try the exotic cuisine, meet the locals, and imbibe the intoxicating sights, sounds, and smells of a new and unfamiliar locale.

But on one or two occasions, a guidebook has elicited the opposite reaction from me. I have actually replanned trips to avoid certain destinations after consulting the travel guide. I won't mention which cities I decided to avoid, but I am grateful for the candor in one guidebook, which supplied a firsthand account of the unfriendliness of the people, the inconvenience of transport, the expense of amenities, and the discomfort of inescapable humidity. I will never know if the report was exaggerated, biased, or blatantly untrue. But I also didn't want to take the chance. If that traveler's experience was half as unappealing as it sounded, I would rather redirect my route in order to visit a more hospitable place.

⊹ NO LAUGHING MATTER ⊹

I also want to explain my use of humor in this, the most sobering of subjects. I take this topic with the utmost seriousness. I am very emotionally invested in the teachings I am drawing upon to create this book, and I shudder to think someone would assume I am flippant or glib about their content. Far from it—the subject disturbs me and haunts me. But when it comes to a subject like this one, we need to take frequent breaks from the heaviness. I mean no irreverence. In these lighter moments, my aim is to give you a sense of relief that you are still enjoying God's gift of life. And my goal is to use levity to sustain you as you encounter the magnanimity of the issue at hand.

Those who know me well could vouch for how seriously I take the subject of Hell and death, but they can also testify that I often cannot get through a funeral sermon without trying to lighten the mood—for my own sake as well as that of my audience.

My hope is that this guide to Hell has that course-changing effect on you! I trust that the details of the afterlife related in this book will help you redirect your route toward a more pleasurable destination.

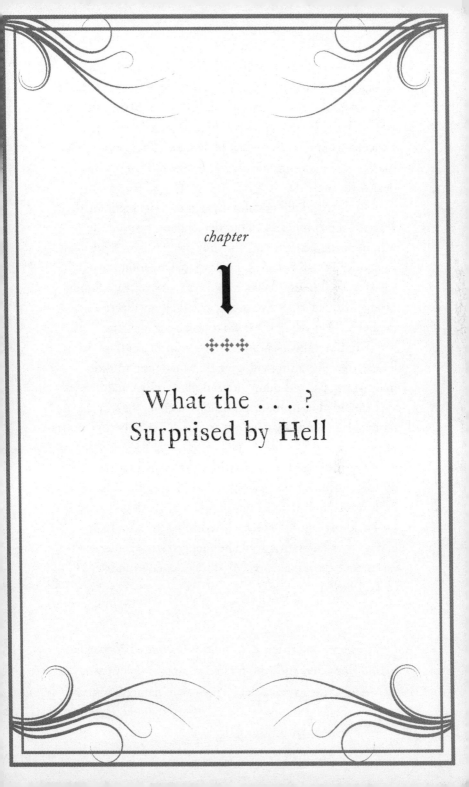

chapter

1

❖❖❖❖

What the . . . ?
Surprised by Hell

I am one of the most well-known people in history, but no one remembers my name. My notoriety is rooted in an account Jesus Christ related to his followers. Many assumed it was a parable—a fictitious story, concocted to illustrate a theological point. But when Jesus said, "There was a rich man . . . ," he was introducing the tragic facts of my life, death, and afterlife.

In a sense, I am grateful my name wasn't mentioned. Imagine my family and all our descendants bearing the weight of shame. After all, the only other person the Bible categorically states went to Hell is Judas Iscariot, the one who betrayed Jesus. Unlike him, I was survived by a family of my own, as well as five brothers and all my nieces and nephews. They never knew what became of me after death.

My funeral was, apparently, a grandiose affair. There were flattering eulogies that made me sound magnanimous, and many offered my family condolences that included customary platitudes such as "he's in a better place" and "may he rest in peace." If only they knew.

The historian Luke recorded my story in his account of the life, times, and teachings of Jesus of Nazareth. When the Bible was compiled under the close scrutiny of Jesus's apostles, the book was called the Gospel According to Luke. Later in history, the narrative would be chopped into chapters and verses, for ease of reference. My story is found in chapter 16, verses 19 to 31:

✦✦✦✦

¹⁹ "There was a rich man who was clothed in purple and fine linen and who feasted sumptuously every day. ²⁰ And at his gate was laid a poor man named Lazarus,

covered with sores, [21] who desired to be fed with what fell from the rich man's table. Moreover, even the dogs came and licked his sores. [22] The poor man died and was carried by the angels to Abraham's side. The rich man also died and was buried, [23] and in Hades, being in torment, he lifted up his eyes and saw Abraham far off and Lazarus at his side. [24] And he called out, 'Father Abraham, have mercy on me, and send Lazarus to dip the end of his finger in water and cool my tongue, for I am in anguish in this flame.' [25] But Abraham said, 'Child, remember that you in your lifetime received your good things, and Lazarus in like manner bad things; but now he is comforted here, and you are in anguish. [26] And besides all this, between us and you a great chasm has been fixed, in order that those who would pass from here to you may not be able, and none may cross from there to us.' [27] And he said, 'Then I beg you, father, to send him to my father's house— [28] for I have five brothers—so that he may warn them, lest they also come into this place of torment.' [29] But Abraham said, 'They have Moses and the Prophets; let them hear them.' [30] And he said, 'No, father Abraham, but if someone goes to them from the dead, they will repent.' [31] He said to him, 'If they do not hear Moses and the Prophets, neither will they be convinced if someone should rise from the dead.' "

✛•✛•✛•✛

There you have it: my legacy. An eternal monument to the folly of false assurance. I was damned by my own folly. And with no one to blame but myself, I am left with no excuses, no arguments, no grounds for appeal, and no hope of release—judgment has been passed, my sentence has been given. My case is closed forever.

I know why Jesus chose me and that poor wretch Lazarus as object lessons. There couldn't have been a more dramatic contrast in the entire world. We were two polar opposite extremes on the prosperity spectrum. I was as rich, healthy, and successful as could be attained in this world. Lazarus was as destitute and sickly as one could fathom. I had everything I wanted; Lazarus had nothing he needed. I was self-made and self-assured. Lazarus was so helpless that he had to be laid at my door in hopes of receiving scraps; he couldn't even walk there himself or ward off the scavenging dogs that prowled our streets at night.

To be honest, I wasn't aware of how badly off that man was. I knew his name. I'd seen him in town; we all had. He was one of the many that money couldn't help. Our streets were lined with beggars. I had given coins to some of them on many occasions, but I knew that even if I gave everything I owned, there would always be poor people in need; even Jesus taught that. So, I figured if I couldn't solve the problem of poverty in our world, why waste too much of my hard-earned money on the poor?

What would a few coins do for this man anyway? He was clearly beyond help. He was so ill that he couldn't walk. Oozing sores spread over his skin so that it hurt to look at him. I actually rationalized my indifference by thinking he must be under God's judgment. If Lazarus were a child of God, surely he would not be left to suffer like that. He must have done something really wicked to deserve such a curse.

I, like many, believed that wealth and health was a sign of God's blessing. I was a prime example of one God was pleased with, or so I thought. I was one of the few that could afford purple linen robes, and only the highest thread-count would do. I ate like a king every single day. My corpulent physique was another sign of God's ample provision. Chubbiness was in style, fortunately for me. I was the envy of every upwardly mobile merchant. My lifestyle was the goal toward which they all strived. Even the religious snobs, the Pharisees, respected me. They saw my prosperity as God's blessing, and it didn't hurt that I supported the local synagogue so generously. That was a good investment, in my mind. After all, why spend money on those God was evidently against, when you can invest in God's work in this world? If I had any sins I had forgotten to repent of, God would surely count my financial contributions in my favor. Oh, how wrong I was.

Death came so quickly that to this day I have no idea what killed my body. Did someone hit me from behind? Was it an aneurism of some sort? One moment I was awake, fit as a horse, and the next I was . . . in this place.

I don't remember how I traveled here. I don't remember seeing the place approaching from a distance. It was instantaneous, like a rude awakening from a vivid dream.

I can admit freely that I was shocked to be in Hell. I had no idea whatsoever that I deserved this sentence; I had no inkling about how bad Hell was. I had always been undecided about whether or not I even believed Hell existed. Eternity was a concept that I couldn't quite get my mind around. And frankly, I didn't bother to try; who wants to think about death and damnation?

It's easier to escape into entertainment, education, career advancement, and other earthly pursuits. These distractions bring fulfillment and happiness; they fill the void and dull the mind. They keep away the dark thoughts of punishment for guilt and the haunting sense of impending justice.

I've been here for probably a couple of thousand years already, but it's as if none of my sentence has been served. There are no fewer days of this torment than there were on the day the punishment started. And I know why. While you might be reeling from the apparent injustice of my state, keep in mind it is only we who are in this place that can truly appreciate how much we deserve it. It is only the damned that can see the necessity for damnation. I have no desire to justify myself, and I certainly don't want anything to do with the God who sent me here. What do I want?

Since I arrived, I have had only two desires, two cravings that never abate. The first is for relief. That's what Jesus was talking about when he told of my begging Abraham for a drop of water. I knew that asking for escape was futile. I just wanted a moment of respite, as if feeling a soothing sensation for one second would give me an eternity of hope.

The second longing I have day and night is this: I want the feeling of worthlessness to go away. I want to warn others about this place. If my physical torment can't allow me to experience relief, then maybe my gnawing conscience can be somewhat salved by helping others avoid this place. It would give my suffering some nobility. I could find a modicum of emotional and spiritual solace if I knew this agony was in the least worthwhile. If one person is persuaded to believe and thus be saved from this, then I could go an eternity knowing my life and death had some redeeming value in this universe.

That is why this memoir exists.

If you are reading this—and this is important—then you must check everything I say against the Bible. The lesson I've learned is that the Bible is the only source that can change minds and hearts, nothing else will work—no argument, no testimony, and not even a miracle are a more authoritative source of truth. So, if this letter directs you to the Bible, then the story Jesus told will have had the purpose he intended: to scare the Hell out of you!

The story of the rich man and Lazarus provides some astounding details about the afterlife. Every idea Jesus touched on in the story is found in his explicit teachings and other passages in the Old and New Testament. But this account pulls those abstract teachings into a Technicolor drama that shocks and informs at the same time.

The word *parable* means "cast alongside." A parable is a story illustrated by plausible true-to-life details (a parable would not contain a talking tortoise and hare that are having a race) that are "cast alongside" a doctrinal truth for the purpose of illustrating reality in an understandable and memorable way. Whether Jesus intended his audience to see this story as an actual account of something that happened or as a tale intended to illustrate an aspect of morality is neither here nor there—the theological truth that he was teaching is the focus.

Each parable had one main point, and in this case it is that health and wealth in this life are not an indication of God's blessing, just as poverty and disease are not a sign of God's displeasure.

That is the main point, but it is the backdrop of the story that is fascinating. The description of what happened is laced with details that are found in many other passages but brought to life in this dramatic story. We will unpack these details throughout the book, but for now let's focus on the unnerving fact that the rich man was actually surprised by Hell.

This rich man was living his luxurious life blithely unaware that it was situated on a fragile layer of ice above the gaping throat of Hell. And he is not alone in his ignorance. The vast majority of people who breathe their last and awake in agony will be shocked beyond their sanity to realize they are no longer on earth, nor in Heaven, but undeniably in the abyss of Hell.

Here are some other passages from Jesus's sermons that underscore the reality that many people who end up in Hell were not expecting to be there.

✞ **Matthew 7:** [22] "On that day many will say to me, 'Lord, Lord, did we not prophesy in your name, and cast out demons in your name, and do many mighty works in your name?' [23] And then will I declare to them, 'I never knew you; depart from me, you workers of lawlessness.'"

✞ **Matthew 13:** [41] The Son of Man will send his angels, and they will gather out of his kingdom all causes of sin and all law-breakers, [42] and throw them into the fiery furnace. In that place there will be weeping and gnashing of teeth.

✣ **Matthew 25: 1–13** recounts the parable of the five foolish virgins who were surprised by the sudden arrival of the groom and disappointed that they couldn't enter the wedding feast.

✣ **Matthew 25: 14–30** is the parable of the talents, where the servant who stashed his master's coin in order not to lose it was surprised that his master was furious that the coin had not been invested properly and was thus taken from him and he was unexpectedly punished.

✣ **Luke 13: 23–28** describes the weeping of realization and the teeth-grinding frustration at not being granted entrance into the kingdom of God: 23 "And someone said to him, 'Lord, will those who are saved be few?' And he said to them, 24 'Strive to enter through the narrow door. For many, I tell you, will seek to enter and will not be able. 25 When once the master of the house has risen and shut the door, and you begin to stand outside and to knock at the door, saying, "Lord, open to us," then he will answer you, "I do not know where you come from." 26 Then you will begin to say, "We ate and drank in your presence, and you taught in our streets." 27 But he will say, "I tell you, I do not know where you come from. Depart from me, all you workers of evil!" 28 In that place there will be weeping and gnashing of teeth, when you see Abraham and Isaac and Jacob and all the prophets in the kingdom of God but you yourselves cast out.' "

All of these people were convinced they would be safe from Hell but were surprised to be damned forever. People rarely believe that they themselves are going to Hell, or they would surely do something to prevent that eventuality. Many employ various means to avoid thinking about the topic altogether. They use entertainment for escape, or arguments and philosophies for an excuse, or religion as a salve for their conscience. But they will be shocked.

Others have thought about the rational necessity for the existence of Hell, but they have convinced themselves that they are safe from such an unthinkable place. It is only by learning about Hell, contemplating it, and deciding to avoid it that we acquire the skills to protect ourselves from the imminent and irreversible danger that it represents.

Jonathan Edwards was the preacher who is credited with preaching the sermon that sparked the eighteenth-century Great Awakening in America—known for being a time of the greatest number of converts to Christianity in the shortest time in U.S. history. That historic sermon, preached on July 8, 1741, at a church in Enfield, Connecticut, was titled "Sinners in the Hands of an Angry God." In one section, he addresses this very idea that the people in Hell are surprised to be there.

❖❖❖❖❖

Almost every natural man that hears of hell, flatters himself that he shall escape it; he depends upon himself for his own security; he flatters himself in what he has done, in what he is now doing, or what he intends to do. Every one lays out matters in his own mind how he shall avoid damnation, and flatters himself that he contrives well for himself . . . each one imagines that he lays out matters better for his own escape than others have done. . . . But the foolish children of men miserably delude themselves in their own schemes, and in confidence in their own strength and wisdom; they trust to nothing but a shadow. . . . If we could speak with them, and inquire of them, one by one, whether they expected, when alive, and when they used to hear about hell, ever to be the subjects of misery, we doubtless, should hear one and another reply, "No, I never intended to come here: I had laid out matters otherwise in my mind; I thought I should contrive well for myself—I thought my scheme good. I intended to take effectual care; but it came upon me unexpected. . . . Death outwitted me: God's wrath was too quick for me. Oh, my cursed foolishness!"

⁜⁜⁜⁜

The reaction to that sermon was reported to include loud wailing, women swooning, and men clinging to pillars for fear the ground would swallow them alive! What was so impactful about that moment—was it the oratory? By all accounts, Edwards read his sermon manuscript in a monotone, lest he be accused of whipping the crowd into an emotional frenzy (a reaction he deplored in any church setting). There is no historical reason we could furnish to explain what happened, except that the people believed what they heard.

These were congregants who had attended church for years and had heard countless sermons. But they were struck by the revelatory reminder that people who end up in Hell consider themselves to be safe until the moment they realize it's too late.

There is a reason that inimitable sermon had such far-reaching impact in the world and through the ages—it forced the audience to contemplate what we all have a natural tendency to avoid thinking about: the possible reality of Hell. Here is another excerpt from the sermon to help us consider what we would naturally prefer to ignore.

✤✤✤

The God that holds you over the pit of hell, much as one holds a spider, or some loathsome insect over the fire, abhors you, and is dreadfully provoked: his wrath toward you burns like fire; he looks upon you as worthy of nothing else, but to be cast into the fire; he is of purer eyes than to bear to have you in his sight; you are ten thousand times more abominable in his eyes, than the most hateful venomous serpent is in ours. You have offended him infinitely more than ever a stubborn rebel did his prince; and yet it is nothing but his hand that holds you from falling into the fire every moment. It is to be ascribed to nothing else, that you did not go to hell the last night; that you was suffered to awake again in this world, after you closed your eyes to sleep.

And there is no other reason to be given, why you have not dropped into hell since you arose in the morning, but that God's hand has held you up. There is no other reason to be given why you have not gone to hell, since you have sat here in the house of God, provoking his pure eyes by your sinful wicked manner of attending his solemn worship. Yea, there is nothing else that is to be given as a reason why you do not this very moment drop down into hell.

O sinner! Consider the fearful danger you are in: it is a great furnace of wrath, a wide and bottomless pit, full of the fire of wrath, that you are held over in the hand of that God, whose wrath is provoked and incensed as much against you, as against many of the damned in hell. You hang by a slender thread, with the flames of divine wrath flashing about it, and ready every moment to singe it, and burn it asunder; and you have no interest in any Mediator, and nothing to lay hold of to save yourself, nothing to keep off the flames of wrath, nothing of your own, nothing that you ever have done, nothing that you can do, to induce God to spare you one moment.

chapter

2

❖❖❖

Why Hell?
A Brief History of Eternity

I attended school in post-colonial South Africa. Picture Harry Potter's alma mater, but without the fun and flying brooms. We had uniforms with blazers and ties, attended a daily assembly where teachers wore academic gowns, lived in fear of corporal punishment, and played cricket. This upbringing was a seedbed of similitudes of Hell. I'm sure a literary titan like Dostoevsky could easily cull numerous metaphors from my school days to craft novels exploring the themes of, say, *time* and punishment.

For example, there were the cricket games. In case you've effectively avoided the misfortune of spectating a cricket game from start to finish, the parts of the event that would most astonish you include the deliberate dullness (both teams wear white, and there is no seventh inning stretch or any other merciful reprieve from boredom), the interminable duration (test matches stretch over five days; each beginning early and pausing at sunset), and sheer pointlessness (these games frequently end in a draw). And this was the fun part of school.

I changed schools several times in my childhood, like a prisoner being transferred from minimum- to maximum-security facilities, so I quickly learned to adapt to the level of discipline that was expected and to rue the consequences that accompanied violations.

In the first grade, the nuns would cane us for tardiness or insubordination, which was called "back-chatting." Their instrument of choice was a thin stick or doweling rod applied crisply to the rear in rapid succession, ranging from one to five blows, corresponding to the level of rebellion. It was proportional punishment, and admittedly, it seemed to be administered fairly (albeit gleefully at times). The part that was unfair, in the evaluation of my seven-year-old sensibilities, was the fact that only boys were punished corporally. Girls had to write lines on the board, or something that seemed equally innocuous, but they were spared physical punishment.

By third grade I was in a relatively civilized institution where retribution for naughtiness involved only punitive P.T. (short for physical training, or "physical torture" as we victims termed it). The P.T. consisted of running laps around the cricket field, pulling weeds from said field for an hour of after-school detention, or sometimes simply doing push-ups until exhaustion. This incorporated psychological duress, as the girls would jeer as they walked by the sweat-sodden victim, adding insult to infamy.

By the time I was a high school English teacher myself, the laws of the country had changed drastically. School faculty was no longer allowed to use any form of corporal punishment. These overdue reforms brought a welcome relief to a system fraught with abuses. But the new restrictions did leave a predictable side effect: rampant insubordination in schools.

It became nearly impossible to enforce any school regulation. Unless the crime was serious enough to warrant expulsion—violence, theft, smoking at school—the "lesser evils" of tardiness, incomplete homework, talking in class, or ignoring a teacher's instructions were performed without the least fear of reprisal. Yes, there was after-school detention after a certain number of demerits had been accumulated, but these indoor, desk-bound sessions were merely a quiet time to do homework that would need to be done anyway. No sweaty weed-pulling allowed.

I think it is fair to say that a law is only as effective as its fair and consistent enforcement. The reason I drive carefully in Los Angeles is because when I moved there, all four times I violated a traffic law the ubiquitous LAPD or CHP or other law enforcement pounced on me. I got tickets for insidious criminal activities like changing lanes without an indicator, using a car-pool lane without a passenger, and the sinister "rolling stop." In Africa, this is considered a polite way to keep the traffic moving along! But in LA, the long arm of the law was never out of reach of my (now) fully-insured, smog-compliant Oldsmobile.

Similarly, the commands of the Bible to love God and obey him can only be taken seriously in light of the warnings of consequences for rejection and disobedience. Without Hell, much in God's universe makes no sense. In practice there would be no fear of contravening any law of God that was not enforced here on earth in some way. In other words, without anticipating a future judgment, people would do whatever they were allowed to do, or whatever they thought they could get away with. The more you remove consequence, the more you undermine accountability and the more you unleash moral inhibitions.

✦ A HISTORY OF HELL ✦

As far back as recorded history takes us, in any and every culture that bothered to write down their beliefs, Hell has haunted mankind. It is not my intention to give a history of how belief in Hell developed in literature, art, and across every religious belief system on the planet. Others have done a fine job of that. But frankly, learning about what different religions believed as well as how and when those doctrines evolved is not as fascinating to me as the fact that they all hold certain aspects in common. Here is a brief sample of some religions' conceptions of Hell. See if you can spot similarities.

- ✦ The Jews know it as *Sheol*, a word referring broadly to the grave, or the realm of the dead, and more ominously as *Gehenna*, named for a fiery garbage dump outside Jerusalem where trash burned day and night, including discarded carcasses of diseased animals, and maggots bred unhindered.

✛ The Greeks believed that in Hades—the underworld populated by departed souls—there was reserved a compartment of frightful torment for those who had somehow displeased one of the divine beings in their pantheon of gods.

✛ Islam's Koran (Qur'an) describes the place of eternal incarceration of infidels, namely *Jahannam*, as comprised of a blazing fire and a dark abyss.

✛ Ancient Egyptians averred that those whose lives were deemed unworthy of a blissful eternity were simply annihilated.

✛ Mayans feared the nine-level realm of *Xibalbá*, including the lower dimensions that were ruled by tormenting spirits.

✛ The Aztecs anticipated a frightening world of prowling jaguars, eternal darkness, and hostile mountains.

✛ Celts called the haunted realm of departed and unsettled spirits *Uffern* (as in the word related to *furnace*).

✛ Slavs named the feared realm of darkness and regret *Peklo*.

✛ In ancient Asian religions, including nascent forms of Shintoism, Hinduism, and other regional spiritualistic sects, names like *Gimokodan* and *Naraka* were employed to describe punitive realms in the afterlife. Even in the understanding of reincarnation a sentence of suffering is executed by a type of "hell-on-earth" demotion to a lesser life form—say a rat, or worm, or (almost as dreadful) a *Dalit* (lower-caste human).

But whatever the moniker assigned to the penal state, certain themes are uncannily congruent: a place or realm that was physically undesirable (either too hot or too cold for comfort), dark or otherwise aesthetically unpleasant, populated by evil spirits that torment those who end up there, and tragically inescapable. Most recognize the banishment to one of these realms is a result of violations of accepted values. It is irreversible once you are deceased, and it is terrifying enough to instill dread while you are still alive.

Positively stated, the purpose of the doctrine seems to be to encourage commitment to the religion's system of avoiding Hell at all costs. Or, to put it more bluntly (and at the risk of sounding glib): the doctrine is meant to scare the Hell out of you.

WHY ON EARTH DO PEOPLE BELIEVE IN HELL?

The concept of Hell is universal. In the history of humanity the belief that there is no afterlife whatsoever is a statistically marginal view. Why is that? What is it about people in this life and on this planet that *needs* Hell?

The answer is that there is something instinctual in human beings that acknowledges that some behavior is good and some bad.

The New Testament puts it this way in Romans 1: "[19] For what can be known about God is plain to them, because God has shown it to them. [20] For his invisible attributes, namely, his eternal power and divine nature, have been clearly perceived, ever since the creation of the world, in the things that have been made. So they are without excuse."

In other words, God has hardwired people with the innate knowledge of what He considers to be right and wrong. A highly educated military general and a primitive tribesman both know that in any culture at any time, the unprovoked torturous murder of an innocent baby (to take one deliberately stomach-churning example) falls squarely into the easily recognized category of evil. No sane person can commit such an act and claim to be ignorant of its moral implications. We know there is right and wrong, and for the most part, we can discern the difference.

And furthermore, even without revelation from God, our brains are predisposed to be consistent. So, you can't believe in good and evil, right and wrong, and concurrently accept that people can do whatever they want with impunity.

Injustice causes cognitive dissonance in our brains, like an unfinished melody, or like a movie where the bad guy escapes. This explains why readers relish the *Count of Monte Cristo* and the revenge Dantès systematically wreaks on each of his enemies who conspired to take all that was precious to him— something in us resonates with the villains getting what they *deserve*.

The doctrine of Hell is one that is not only clearly taught in the Bible but also is demanded by practical, philosophical, and theological necessity.

Practical Necessity for Hell

Our first passengers to get off this bus ride to explore the disturbing doctrines of Hell will likely be the atheist who would assume this was a trip with no destination. Atheists don't believe in Hell because they don't believe in the afterlife. Practically speaking, for an atheist, there is really no reason to do the right thing unless there is some level of incentive or enforcement in the here and now or a personal moral compass that drives a concern for others. This explains why atheists in regions with effective policing, moral upbringing, and social pressure to behave decently tend to be nice people who do good, abide by the law, and contribute to society. If one doesn't bring a tart to the community potluck but gorges oneself on the neighbors' dishes, then even if you were able to live with the feelings of guilt, you would be wary of never again getting invited.

But in parts of the world where civil and even criminal laws go unenforced, such as in some war-torn regions throughout the world, and sadly even in many cities in my home country of South Africa, there are people who fear no consequence for their crimes in this life due to ineffective enforcement, nor do they have any concern about judgment in the afterlife.

You may think that conscience would be enough for a person to do the right thing, but remember that your conscience is informed by your society, your family, your education, and your beliefs. These are very subjective factors. For people in another part of the world, their family may teach them violent revenge as a form of restoring honor after being verbally insulted. In that same country they may have been taught that power, not virtue, is the only way to be respected and that an act is only a crime if you get caught.

In the Zulu culture, power is the highest virtue. Getting away with a crime is considered to be a sign of strength, not of moral weakness. This can be illustrated by a Zulu man winning a presidential election by landslide margins, shortly after publicized trials for rape and corruption, and while illegally practicing polygamy! It seems morality as we understand it breaks down in any place and time where doing the right thing is not a legal requirement. Consider Nazi Germany's laws concerning the treatment of Jews or America's laws concerning slavery before the Civil War. What was legal is now illegal. Does that make it right then and wrong now?

The practical reasons for morality also implode when the social requirements are removed. Think of how adultery was highly frowned upon in Britain in the 1930s, which led to the abdication of Edward VIII for pursuing marriage with his mistress, Mrs. Wallis Simpson, who was a divorced woman and in the throes of a second divorce while flaunting her torrid affair with the King of England. Now compare that with the American electorate's verdict that Bill Clinton's adulterous sex life was no reason for him to resign as president. Is adultery right or wrong? It depends on whom you ask and when you ask them. The notions of ethics and morality in Hawthorne's *The Scarlet Letter* seem positively puritanical today. And indeed they are, but puritanical is an adjective embraced by many Protestant Evangelical Christians today, with connotations of virtue and moral uprightness, while being a term of derision to many others. It's all relative.

There really is no sense in saying that people should "do the right thing" in general, because the "right thing" is whatever your situation deems right. This is why, at the heart of the practical problem there is a philosophical one.

The Philosophical Reason for Hell

Philosophically, the need for there to be a Hell if there is a Heaven is unavoidable. The core of the philosophical problem is surreptitiously lurking in the phrase I have been bandying about: "doing the right thing."

At least atheists are consistent; they acknowledge neither Heaven nor Hell. But for them, there is no higher power that dictates what the "right thing" or "wrong thing" to do might be. So, for practical purposes, those who do not believe in God must construct their own morality based on what is "acceptable" behavior in a particular environment. It's right because it's right in our society at our time, but it's not right because there is a metaphysical, objective standard of ethics that rewards good and punishes evil.

In the West, physically assaulting your wife might get you arrested, and at the very least, anyone who finds out about it will look down on you. But in a Middle Eastern village I visited, it was considered socially disgraceful to *not* slap your wife publicly if she had humiliated you. Is that simply "different strokes for different folks" or a ghastly perversion of society's expectations? You decide.

If a person is okay with saying that genocide, adultery, necrophilia, and pedophilia could be acceptable in some cases because of the cultural norms and values that tolerate such behavior, then I would award them points for consistency. But I wouldn't want them around my kids or anywhere near my dead body. (And yes, all of those behaviors have been legal and accepted at various times in various cultures or subcultures in history.)

I hope you waved good-bye to the atheists; most would have lost interest in our tour and left the trip to Hell and caught the first bus to reality. For those still curious enough to remain with us, let's delve further into the philosophical reason for the existence of Hell.

Those of us who do not believe that right and wrong are relative are forced to admit that behavior can be wrong even if you get away with it, and we anticipate injustice being set straight. It seems fair that an unjust act that is never punished in this life must be punished in the next.

An action is only as "wrong" as much as it calls for proportional punishment. If you don't quite agree with that, answer me this: Which is more wrong, speeding or murder? The justice for speeding is a monetary fine; usually it is not a debilitating amount, just enough to sting a bit. The justice for murder is lengthy, sometimes lifetime, incarceration or even the death penalty. If a judge let the murderer off with a small cash fine, we would surely call that judge unjust and say that justice has not been done.

So, what about the actions *God* sees as really bad? Can God be known for his justice if he neglects to punish actions he has deemed as wrong? Of course not. To be a just and righteous judge, God himself is a theological necessity and must punish wrongdoing in some way.

The Bible calls wrong behavior *sin*. A sin is not necessarily a crime. It is not a crime to gossip, but it is considered wrong behavior in the Bible. It is a sin. The same goes for adultery, for example. It's legal, though usually socially repugnant. But fornication (sleeping together before marriage) is neither illegal nor socially stigmatic in many parts of the world today, though this was not always the case—just read *The Scarlet Letter* or watch *Downton Abbey* to get a taste of how distasteful being caught in fornication used to be.

Whether or not the biblical catalogue of sins is authoritative is a matter of intense debate in religious circles. But for the sake of the argument, let us assume for now that there is a God who is a moral being, who determines what is good and evil, and who has revealed his will to mankind in the Bible.

Even without the scriptural revelation about Hell, there is a theological necessity for it. If God says something is wrong, but people do it with impunity in this life—for example, lusting sexually after any person you are not married to or coveting your neighbor's Porsche—then there must be some way for God to enforce that law, or it is as effective as the no-smoking sign in a burning building.

In other words, it is not theologically consistent for a person to believe in a moral God, and Heaven, but not Hell.

Enter the Universalist. Universalists believe that there is a Heaven and that everyone goes there. I am grateful for the generosity, since it means that even if they are right and I'm wrong, either way I get to go to Heaven. However, I'm afraid it's not their motives I question but their logical consistency.

If you believe everyone ends up in Heaven, then you need to realize that your view, stated more bluntly, could be worded this way: "A man who kidnaps a child, rapes her, tortures her for years, and eventually kills her has exactly the same blissful reward after his death as the victim of that heinous atrocity." Whatever the alternative to Heaven is like (whether you call it Hell, Sheol, or Naraka), a belief in any type of afterlife "reward" is to necessarily believe in a corresponding afterlife "lack of reward." Or, as in many cases, an "anti-reward." Jehovah's Witnesses, for example, hold that anyone who does not inherit eternal life in Heaven or on the New Earth (Paradise) is simply annihilated— and annihilation isn't an active punishment, but simply a lack of a reward. Again, I appreciate their merciful view, and if I am wrong and they are right, then I won't live past death to find out.

The pressing question when it comes to a punitive afterlife is what the nature of that anti-reward is. Is it a mild "study-hall level" of detention, or a physical torture of conscious eternal torment, or is it the blissful oblivion of annihilation? That is the subject of later chapters. For now, we only need to acknowledge that if there is neither reward nor punishment in the afterlife, then all morality is utterly relative, and that anything that is morally repulsive, from slavery and genocide to murder and child molestation, is permissible morally if the culture, time, and place deem it to be so.

In that scenario there is no absolute right or wrong to be set straight at judgment day. It is up to the law, society, and other enforcement systems here and now to determine what will be punished and what will not. More often than not, whatever is caught and deemed punishable is punished. Otherwise there is no consequence for depravity, no matter how reprehensible it seems to you personally.

However, if there is an afterlife accountability, and if some things are wrong whether they are legal and socially acceptable or not, then there is not an equal and benign reward awaiting everyone.

The Theological Necessity for Hell

The third reason people believe in Hell is the theological necessity. If there is a God and he has revealed what his will is and people continually violate that will, then there must be a way for him to remain just and holy and morally good. If there is no Hell, then the concept of God as he reveals himself in the Bible is utterly inconsistent.

The pouting psalmist, a man called Asaph who composed Psalm 73, teased out this theme eloquently. In this psalm, Asaph is bewailing how unjust the world seems to him. He is a person who strives diligently to please God. He keeps God's laws; he follows God's ways; he loves God and enjoys a relationship with God as his Savior and Lord and King.

"So," Asaph asks bitterly, "why is it that I am poor, starving, exploited, and vulnerable, while my wicked God-hating rival is so rich that he is fat from food? The wicked guy is well groomed, respected, and ensconced in luxury despite his violent acts and blasphemy. What is going on?"

⁘⊹⊹⊹⊹

Psalm 73: [3] For I was envious of the arrogant when I saw the prosperity of the wicked. [4] For they have no pangs until death; their bodies are fat and sleek. [5] They are not in trouble as others are; they are not stricken like the rest of mankind. [6] Therefore pride is their necklace; violence covers them as a garment. [7] Their eyes swell out through fatness; their hearts overflow with follies. [8] They scoff and speak with malice; loftily they threaten oppression. [9] They set their mouths against the heavens, and their tongue struts through the earth. [10] Therefore his people turn back to them, and find no fault in them. [11] And they say, "How can God know? Is there knowledge in the Most High?" [12] Behold, these are the wicked; always at ease, they increase in riches.

⊹⊹⊹⊹

Asaph is articulating one of the age-old conundrums in life: If God is good and powerful, why is there evil in the world? Why do Christians go poor and persecuted and lose business and get mugged, while people who reject Jesus seem to do just fine in life? In fact they do better financially because they are not limited by scruples or hindered by conscience. What is the profit in being a Christian at all?

Asaph says, basically, "God, what is the point of me being on your team if you bless the bad guys and curse me!? Is this religion thing all in vain?"

[13] All in vain have I kept my heart clean and washed my hands in innocence. [14] For all the day long I have been stricken and rebuked every morning.

But then something happens. Asaph gives himself a wake-up call and gets control of his runaway thoughts. He admits to himself, *When I gave it some thought I realized that their judgment is coming in the future.* In other words, he "discerned their end":

[16] But when I thought how to understand this, it seemed to me a wearisome task, [17] until I went into the sanctuary of God; then I discerned their end. [18] Truly you set them in slippery places; you make them fall to ruin. [19] How they are destroyed in a moment, swept away utterly by terrors!

Suddenly there is a massive swing in tone, attitude, and perspective, when the psalmist shifts his gaze toward the future judgment, what he calls the "end of the wicked." And not only does Asaph recognize the afterlife consequence or "end" of the wicked, but he also gains perspective about his own reward and glory that comes not necessarily in this life but after judgment day:

[24] You guide me with your counsel, and afterward you will receive me to glory. [25] Whom have I in heaven but you? And there is nothing on earth that I desire besides you. . . . [27] For behold, those who are far from you shall perish; you put an end to everyone who is unfaithful to you. [28] But for me it is good to be near God; I have made the Lord God my refuge, that I may tell of all your works.

The dénouement of the psalm brings encouraging closure. Belief in Heaven and Hell is what makes sense of God's world here and now. All the evil that goes unpunished in this world must be dealt with in the next. And all the victimization that goes unchecked will be set straight.

The Biblical Necessity of Hell

Some people I've met claim to love the stories of Jesus Christ— the promise of Heaven, the hope of salvation, the comfort of forgiveness, and its timeless wisdom—while simultaneously rejecting the notion of Hell, the concept of sin, and the warnings of a coming judgment. They treat the Bible like a theological buffet table, picking and choosing what to believe according to their personal tastes.

But the Bible was not written that way. It claims to be an authoritative, comprehensive, and holistic word from God to his creation. For those who accept this, the reality of Hell in Scripture is undeniable.

Jesus said it this way to the rich man:

❖•❖•❖

Luke 16: [25] But Abraham said, "Child, remember that you in your lifetime received your good things, and Lazarus in like manner bad things; but now he is comforted here, and you are in anguish."

❖•❖•❖

This great reversal that could be expected in the afterlife was a recurring theme of Christ's preaching.

✢ **Matthew 11:** [11] Truly, I say to you, among those born of women there has arisen no one greater than John the Baptist. Yet the one who is least in the kingdom of heaven is greater than he.

✢ **Matthew 19:** [29] And everyone who has left houses or brothers or sisters or father or mother or children or lands, for my name's sake, will receive a hundredfold and will inherit eternal life. [30] But many who are first will be last, and the last first.

✢ **Matthew 20:** [15] Am I not allowed to do what I choose with what belongs to me? Or do you begrudge my generosity?' [16] So the last will be first, and the first last.

✢ **Mark 10:** [29] Jesus said, "Truly, I say to you, there is no one who has left house or brothers or sisters or mother or father or children or lands, for my sake and for the gospel, [30] who will not receive a hundredfold now in this time, houses and brothers and sisters and mothers and children and lands, with persecutions, and in the age to come eternal life. [31] But many who are first will be last, and the last first."

✢ **Luke 13:** ²⁷ But he will say, "I tell you, I do not know where you come from. Depart from me, all you workers of evil!" ²⁸ In that place there will be weeping and gnashing of teeth, when you see Abraham and Isaac and Jacob and all the prophets in the kingdom of God but you yourselves cast out. ²⁹ And people will come from east and west, and from north and south, and recline at table in the kingdom of God. ³⁰ And behold, some are last who will be first, and some are first who will be last.

The doctrine of Hell is unavoidable. We need it practically to curb our innate bent to self-destructive and antisocial behavior. We need it to logically make sense of our ethics, morality, and sense of justice. And we need Hell to reconcile our idea of a holy, just, and good God as he is revealed in Scripture.

Without a belief in an afterlife of justice, much of the unpunished evil in this life simply doesn't make sense. The hopelessness of Hell gives us hope that a life spent in a right relationship with God is not meaningless. And that is why, in a very real sense, people on earth need Hell to be real.

Of course, something is not real just because it makes sense for it to be real. There must be some sort of evidence for us to be convinced. This is where our sightseeing trip around Hell now takes us—to what the Bible says about Hell. We are about to witness what Hell is really like. I hope you dressed light, because it's about to get really, really hot in here.

chapter

3

❖❖❖

To Hell and Back:
Who Has the T-Shirt?

In Chapter 2 we discussed why people believe in Hell. We saw how the vast majority of people who have ever lived possessed a belief in the existence of a punitive afterlife. We also saw that Hell as a doctrine makes sense out of practical religious life, creates logical consistency in a philosophy of ethics, and forms theological consistency in our understanding of God. But just because something is believed by most people and makes perfect sense is not proof that its existence is certain. Just think of ether.

✣ FAITH IN ETHER ✣

Philosopher René Descartes had some trouble trusting his senses. He coined the quintessential philosophical maxim "I think, therefore I am" because the only thing you can ever be sure even exists is yourself, since you are the one thinking that cockamamie thought. Everything and everyone else in the universe could be a figment of your imagination (or a product of the Matrix!), but that would only prove that you had an imagination, and as the thinker you are thus the only one who certainly exists.

I find it amusing that Descartes also wholeheartedly bought into the notion of "luminiferous æther" (or ether).

Æther is the putative "substance" that was universally believed—by everyone from the literate third-grader to the father of physics, Sir Isaac Newton himself—to occupy every nook and cranny of outer space. Since light behaves like a wave, it must have a substance through which to move from the stars to earth. This "proved" that space was not a vacuum. Scientists described ether as invisible and weightless, causing no friction or any other effect that would prove its existence. Convenient.

And because the quirky quantum physicists hadn't yet

thrown their revolutionary curveball at all things Newtonian by proving light also had a particle nature, there was no way to prove otherwise. The scientific community lapped up the theory of ether like a thirsty, gullible puppy for centuries until the twentieth century, when it was proven that it simply did not exist.

But after this auspicious theory had been outed as no more than a figment of the academy's imagination, many of the cognoscenti were nonplussed that they could have been proven so horrendously wrong. Years after incontrovertible evidence had been furnished, British physicist Sir J. J. Thompson, who won the Nobel Prize for discovering the electron, pertinaciously averred: "Ether is not a fantastic creation of the speculative philosopher, but it is as essential to us as the air we breathe." Indeed.

Faith is a funny thing. All of life and living is lubricated by faith. Every time you sit on a chair, brush your teeth, drop your kid off at school, or read a blog, you are trusting someone or something.

But what about your soul? Do you trust that your pastor is right? Do you trust what your parents taught you? Do you trust what you saw in a documentary or heard during your pot-smoking college roommate's stoned pontification? What would you trust as a source of information about Hell?

ROUND TRIP?
CLAIMS AT HAVING RETURNED

In Greek mythology, there were a few mortals who returned from Hades, the underworld. One such revenant hero was Orpheus. He was renowned for his mesmerizing musical ability. As the story goes, Orpheus's love for his deceased wife, Eurydice, prompted him to make a journey to the realm of death. He then charmed Hades with his music and requested that Hades allow Eurydice to return with him to life. Under the spell of Orpheus's song, Hades acquiesced to the plea. However, he specified one condition: that Orpheus lead the way back home and not once look back until the couple were both in the land of the living. In his anticipation, the moment Orpheus entered life he looked back, only to see his beloved Eurydice instantly whisked back into the underworld because of his lack of faith.

There are a handful of would-be Orpheuses today. These putative return-ticket holders have claimed to have been to Hell and back, literally. They claim to have died, witnessed the horrors of the netherworld, and then somehow returned to publish a book about it, soul and sanity intact.

I cry, "Foul." In fact, I cry, "Hogwash!"

If their claim is true, then the Bible's is not. And frankly, the credentials of Jesus Christ and his chosen prophets are hard to match.

According to the Bible, those who are forgiven of their sins never get anywhere near Hell, and those who die unforgiven never get a second chance, or even the smallest reprieve from their punishment. A weekend bivouac to Hell is simply not one of the travel packages God offers. No one can escape because part of the definition of Hell is that it is a place absent of God's grace, mercy, and forgiveness. And therefore it is necessarily a place of no hope.

If people could expect to die, be judged for their sins, sentenced to Hell, and then somehow obtain a second chance and a book deal, then that would be unprecedented. This occurrence would be a source of God's grace, mercy, hope, and forgiveness, so as a result, this final destination would not be as final as the Bible says. If tales of cheating death were true, the biblical definition of Hell would be compromised.

GONE FOR GOOD:
THE CHASM BETWEEN HEAVEN AND HELL

Remember the rich man's request to receive mercy in the form of a single drop of water from Heaven? He was denied for two reasons: one, he was getting his just desserts; and two, receiving mercy from Heaven while in Hell is not even possible:

✢✢✢

Luke 16: [25] But Abraham said, "Child, remember that you in your lifetime received your good things, and Lazarus in like manner bad things; but now he is comforted here, and you are in anguish. [26] And besides all this, between us and you a great chasm has been fixed, in order that those who would pass from here to you may not be able, and none may cross from there to us."

✢✢✢

Even believers from the Old Testament knew this. Job, who was the victim of unspeakable suffering in this life, was privy to some profound insight about the afterlife. He declares,

✢✢✢

Job 7: [5] My flesh is clothed with worms and dirt; my skin hardens, then breaks out afresh. [6] My days are swifter than a weaver's shuttle and come to their end without hope. [7] "Remember that my life is a breath; my eye will never again see good. [8] The eye of him who sees me will behold me no more; while your eyes are on me, I shall be gone. ⁹As the cloud fades and vanishes, so he who goes down to Sheol does not come up; ¹⁰he returns no more to his house, nor does his place know him anymore.

✦✦✦✦

Job knew what Jesus knew: no one who goes to Hell gets to return, and no one back home can contact the damned. There is a great divide between Heaven and Hell that prevents a transfer of address. And earth is not a station on the way between the two. Escape from Hell even for a day would be far more mercy than is allowed.

Why would a person claim otherwise? I don't know. But I can think of three possible reasons. People who have claimed to go to Hell and back could be (a) lying for attention or money, (b) deluded and hallucinating, or (c) messing with you.

DIRTY ROTTEN SCOUNDRELS: DEMONS LIE . . . A LOT

There is another source from which some claimants draw their information: demons. Demons are, according the Bible, erstwhile angelic beings who were permanently cast out of Heaven for their role in Satan's rebellion against God. They are creatures that have irrevocably fallen from grace and spend their existence wreaking turmoil in the lives of human beings. They hate that humans are God's favored creatures, and they are consummately deceptive. The very word the Scriptures use to name them, *devils* (a translation of the Greek *diabolos*), means "liar." Other words for Satan and his henchmen include "Adversary," "Slanderer," and "Accuser." Demons are described as "lying spirits," "tormenting spirits," and are said to work for Satan, the "Father of Lies."

Okay, so would you trust anything you heard from a demon? It would be like seeking investment advice from a convicted con artist. Demons are—to borrow a phrase from a classic 1980s comedy—dirty rotten scoundrels. I wouldn't trust a demon as far as I could vomit.

Stranger Than Fiction: Imagination Is Not Information

People also rely upon fiction to inform their conception of what Hell is like. Yes, you read that right. If you had to take a moment and visualize Hell, your imagination would likely be informed by movies you've watched, novels you've read, and art you've seen. You may have studied Dante's *Inferno* while in college or seen Raphael's illustrations in museums or on book covers.

Frank Perretti is a best-selling science fiction author who writes for a Christian readership. He injects copious doses of poetic license in his depictions of demons and their operations. He doesn't claim to be postulating a doctrinal viewpoint; he is writing a fanciful story. And yet even Christians fall into the trap of superimposing what they visualize in his novels on top of what they read in the Bible.

And of course, the proliferation of vampire pulp fiction is also in vogue. When one finds a teen pried away from her smartphone long enough to read an actual book, it is not surprising to see the cover depicting some tortured romantic triangle between a mortal, a vampire, and a werewolf.

And then there are the TV series, like *Charmed*, *Angel*, *Supernatural*, and other weekly doses of speculative oddities and contorted plot lines about saving the world from colorful characters who hail from the netherworld. Movies that feature glimpses at a mythological conception of Hell include classics like

Ghostbusters, *Hellboy*, *The Devil's Advocate*, *Constantine*, and *The Underworld*. These blockbusters and others all capitalize on our fascination with the unknown.

Naturally, the depictions of these writers and directors rarely attempt to correlate with any biblical revelation at all. Not that they need to—they aren't claiming to be documentaries. But viewers sometimes cannot help integrating what they've seen or read into what they believe. This leaves our view of something extremely important infused with fiction and resulting in a mongrelized hybrid of truth and error.

✛ WHO WROTE THE BOOK ON HELL? ✛

Though everyone will have their own favorite source of authority for matters pertaining to life and the afterlife, it's hard to beat the Old and New Testaments when it comes to time-honored acceptance, historical credibility, literary cohesiveness, and scholastic approval.

✛ WAS JESUS EVER IN HELL? ✛

One fascinating question is whether Jesus himself ever witnessed Hell firsthand. Some teach that when Jesus died he spent the three days before his resurrection in Hell, being tortured by Satan as he suffered for the sin of the world. This is a misunderstanding of what the Bible teaches about Christ's sufferings. When he died, Jesus said, "It is finished" in reference to the atoning work on the cross. His suffering for mankind ended at that moment. The debt of sin mankind owes is to God the Father, not Satan. And the price of Christ's death was paid voluntarily to God the Father, to satisfy his sense of justice and wrath against sin while simultaneously fulfilling his love for mankind, making forgiveness possible. Satan had nothing to do with it.

The Bible also makes it clear that Jesus went to Paradise for the three days before returning. But there is a passage that gives us a hint as to the one time Jesus went to a place of punishment—not to suffer, but to proclaim victory.

❖❖❖❖

1 Peter 3: [18] For Christ also suffered once for sins, the righteous for the unrighteous, that he might bring us to God, being put to death in the flesh but made alive in the spirit, [19] in which he went and proclaimed to the spirits in prison, [20] because they formerly did not obey, when God's patience waited in the days of Noah, while the ark was being prepared, in which a few, that is, eight persons, were brought safely through water.

❖❖❖❖

This is referring to a group of demons who were already incarcerated in the abyss, being kept away from the earth until their final condemnation on judgment day. A possible explanation is that these are the demons referred to by the New Testament writer Jude.

❖❖❖❖

Jude 1: [6] And the angels [fallen angels, that is, demons] who did not stay within their own position of authority, but left their proper dwelling, he has kept in eternal chains under gloomy darkness until the judgment of the great day. . . .

❖❖❖❖

This also explains why demons who encountered Jesus while he was on earth freaked out and begged not to be locked up, like in this dramatic account in Luke 8.

Luke 8: [27] When Jesus had stepped out on land, there met him a man from the city who had demons. For a long time he had worn no clothes, and he had not lived in a house but among the tombs. [28] When he saw Jesus, he cried out and fell down before him and said with a loud voice, "What have you to do with me, Jesus, Son of the Most High God? I beg you, do not torment me." [29] For he had commanded the unclean spirit to come out of the man. (For many a time it had seized him. He was kept under guard and bound with chains and shackles, but he would break the bonds and be driven by the demon into the desert.) [30] Jesus then asked him, "What is your name?" And he said, "Legion," for many demons had entered him. [31] And they begged him not to command them to depart into the abyss. [32] Now a large herd of pigs was feeding there on the hillside, and they begged him to let them enter these. So he gave them permission. [33] Then the demons came out of the man and entered the pigs, and the herd rushed down the steep bank into the lake and were drowned.

Wow. That's what we call "deviled ham"! The lesson we learn is that (a) demons respond to Jesus's authority, (b) demons can possess and physically control animals as well as certain humans, and (c) demons are petrified of being prematurely cast into the abyss like their unlucky compatriots, who Jude says are already bound there awaiting their sentence.

To sum it up: no, Jesus never went to Hell, and certainly not to suffer. He went to the abyss to declare victory over the demons already imprisoned there. But those demons are not yet sentenced to Hell—they're just awaiting their verdict from a holding cell.

If you are reeling a bit from the at-times confusing bureaucracy associated with the great abyss, that's okay. Our next chapter will help straighten all of that out as we learn about the lay of the land in the netherworld. Think of it as discovering the suburbs of Hell.

chapter

4

❖❖❖

Downtown Abyss:
Learning the Lay of the Land

I don't mean to be disparaging of anyone else's favorite literature, but some tabloid magazines seem to go out of their way to invite ridicule. Some sources of information about Hell are obviously more reliable than others.

How much credibility would you attribute to a tabloid? Probably zero. And yet, one popular meme achieved inordinate traction in the media when a tabloid published a photograph of a plume of smoke that allegedly resembled a devilish face. The article claimed the mile-deep Alaskan oil well emitted a sulfurous odor, white-hot flames, and somehow led to suspicions that the drillers had inadvertently punctured Hell. The story grew wings when Alaska's governor apparently conceded that the event may be a case of the Devil playing tricks in order to side with terrorists who also desired America to run out of oil. Another eminent senator was quoted as citing the incident as a warning of the unpredictability of oil drilling. He cautioned that the effects could have long-term consequences, both environmental and biblical. I'm not making this up.

This far-fetched urban legend has been pinballed around inboxes of the gullible since the 1990s. It first emerged as a story about "The Well to Hell," which was a deep borehole well drilled in Russia. The crew apparently lowered a super-heat-resistant microphone into the pit and recorded sounds of damned souls screaming. Yup. Thankfully the farce has petered out somewhat and has been debunked. The sounds turned out to be a retooled horror movie soundtrack. Though it was true that the Soviet Union sunk an eight-mile deep borehole on the Kola Peninsula in 1989, the only anomalies recorded were geological, not supernatural. The temperature is what curtailed the project, but they peaked at about 180 degrees Centigrade (360 degrees Fahrenheit)—as hot as the temperature of your oven, not a furnace in Hell's kitchen.

The story was eagerly lapped up by American tabloids and then got a major PR boost when Trinity Broadcasting Network ran the story as "proof" that Hell is real. (Most Christians believe the Bible is sufficient proof without collaboration from the Soviets or tabloids, but there you go.)

So, for the purposes of this book, do we dismiss every aspect of this report? Um, yes.

And yet, Russian boreholes notwithstanding, the episode exhibits the fact that many people insist that Hell is not merely a state of mind but a real place. So is it? Could we one day secure the coordinates of Hell and maybe get Google Earth to capture it for us to view from the safety of our laptops? Yes and no.

✦ THE STATE HELL IS IN ✦

The three most important aspects of real estate and the afterlife: location, location, location. It is essential that we disabuse ourselves of the misconception that the nature of Hell is unknowable because it is a merely "spiritual reality" or a "state of mind."

For example, Pope John Paul II, in a live audience address given on July 28, 1999, opined that "Rather than a place, Hell indicates the state of those who freely and definitively separate themselves from God, the source of all life and joy." He didn't supply any biblical backing to that view, which is one of the unique job perks of the papacy: the prerogative of infallible proclamation: "It is so because I said so."

Incidentally, previous infallible popes, and even a recent successor, Benedict XVI, clarified that "Jesus came to tell us that he wants us all in Heaven, and that Hell, of which so little is said in our time, exists and is eternal for those who close their hearts to his love."

On the other end of the Catholic-Protestant divide, the ex-evangelical Rob Bell declared in characteristically slippery language: "[Hell is] a word that refers to the big, wide, terrible evil that comes from the secrets hidden deep without our hearts all the way to the massive, society-wide collapse and chaos that comes when we fail to live in God's world God's way."

So, according to Bell: Hell is the stuff that bugs you and messes up this world but not a place dead people go.

But the Bible describes Hell only in terms of it being a place. The story in Luke 16 uses unequivocally spatial language of "from here" and "to there" and "between us." The nameless rich man dies and recognizes he is trapped in a "place" (Luke 16:28) that is physically removed from the realm of comfort where Abraham and Lazarus reside. He is informed that he is bound to that location.

And yet, that location is not geographic in the sense that it is in our realm (or what Stephen Hawking would call "our dimension"). So, no, Google Maps wouldn't be of any help, nor would Russian drilling crews.

✦ WHERE IS HELL? ✦

In a word, Hell is . . . down. Do I mean that if we had the technology we could explore the earth's core and stumble upon a street sign marked "Hades"? No. Hell, though it is described in spatial and physical terms, is still a realm that spirits, but not matter, inhabit. The Bible and many other religions consistently refer to the location of this realm in terms of a universal "descent motif" or "katabasis." That's book club argot indicating Hell is always said to be "down." They don't call it the underworld for nothing.

Here are some examples from the Bible:

✦ **Job 17:** [16] Will it go down to the bars of Sheol? Shall we descend together into the dust?"

✢ **Romans 10:** [7] . . . "Who will descend into the abyss?" (that is, to bring Christ up from the dead).

✢ **Ephesians 4:** [9] In saying, "He ascended," what does it mean but that he had also descended into the lower regions, the earth? [10] He who descended is the one who also ascended far above all the heavens, that he might fill all things.

✢ **Psalm 55:** [15] Let death steal over them; let them go down to Sheol alive; for evil is in their dwelling place and in their heart.

✢ **Proverbs 7:** [27] Her house is the way to Sheol, going down to the chambers of death.

✢ **Isaiah 14:** [11] Your pomp is brought down to Sheol, the sound of your harps; maggots are laid as a bed beneath you, and worms are your covers. . . . [15] But you are brought down to Sheol, to the far reaches of the pit.

✢ **Luke 10:** [15] And you, Capernaum, will you be exalted to heaven? You shall be brought down to Hades.

This identification of Hell as being "down" is meant to be an unmistakable contrast with the other spiritual realm, Heaven, which is always said to be—you guessed it—"up."

✢ **2 Corinthians 12:** [2] I know a man in Christ who fourteen years ago was caught up to the third heaven—whether in the body or out of the body I do not know, God knows. [3] And I know that this man was caught up into paradise—whether in the body or out of the body I do not know, God knows—

✢ **Luke 24:** [51] While he [Jesus] blessed them, he parted from them and was carried up into heaven.

✢ **Revelation 11:** [12] Then they heard a loud voice from heaven saying to them, "Come up here!" And they went up to heaven in a cloud, and their enemies watched them.

Every indication of Heaven is that it is up, and every indication of Hell is that it is down, which explains why the rich man looked up from Hades and saw into Heaven. I take this as God accommodating human language to emphasize the incompatibility of these two worlds. The Oxford professor and renowned Christian apologist (and yes, children's book author) C. S. Lewis disagreed with the sentiment William Blake expressed in his book *The Marriage of Heaven and Hell*. Unlike Blake, Lewis believes that there never was, and never will be, a marriage between Heaven and Hell—rather, they represent a great divorce. This is why the Bible portrays the one location as unambiguously removed from the other. One is as *down* as you can fathom, and one is as up as can be.

We will not find either place with an intergalactic satellite probe or a subterranean drilling droid. There is a reason you leave your body behind when you die. Your body's matter cannot traverse to the afterlife dimension. Your soul separates and enters the spiritual realm, while your disposable body gets recycled as fertilizer.

What is interesting is that the description of Hell is consummately spatial, and even involves terminology used to designate various areas or regions within Hell. There are hints at levels of punishment in Hell, as well as distinct sectors, or, as I think of them, suburbs of Hell.

✦ THE SIGN ON HELL'S GATE: SHEOL/HADES ✦

It may surprise you to learn that the Bible uses specific terminology to refer to the various locations in the afterlife. For example, what most people refer to as "Heaven," the Bible actually subdivides into Paradise (also called the third Heaven), the New Heavens, and New Earth. Likewise, what most people call "Hell" or *Sheol*, the Bible slices into *Gehenna* and *Tartarus*. It helps to know Greek.

Hades in Greek usually refers generically to death, but in the Bible it designates the place where condemned souls are sent. In the Hebrew of the Old Testament, the equivalent term is Sheol, also meaning "the grave" or death in general, but sometimes specifically indicating the holding place of the condemned.

Within Sheol/Hades there is a place called *Gehenna* and another place called the abyss, or *Tartarus*.

The Temporary Holding Cell for Humans:
Gehenna

Gehenna (presenting in the New Testament as a direct Greek transliteration of the Aramaic word) is where the unrighteous go immediately when they die, like the rich man in Luke 16.

The Temporary Prison for Demons:
The Abyss/*Tartarus*

Tartarus is a Greek word that is more specific than Hades, and refers to an abyss where some demons have been locked away, and where Satan will in the future be bound for a thousand years.

+ **2 Peter 2:** [4] For if God did not spare angels when they sinned, but cast them into hell [that is, *Tartarus*] and committed them to chains of gloomy darkness to be kept until the judgment;

+ **Luke 8:** [30] Jesus then asked him [a demon-possessed man], "What is your name?" And he said, "Legion," for many demons had entered him. [31] And they begged him not to command them to depart into the abyss.

✠ **Revelation 20:** ¹Then I saw an angel coming down from heaven, holding in his hand the key to the bottomless pit and a great chain. ² And he seized the dragon, that ancient serpent, who is the devil and Satan, and bound him for a thousand years, ³ and threw him into the pit, and shut it and sealed it over him, so that he might not deceive the nations any longer, until the thousand years were ended. After that he must be released for a little while.

The Lake of Fire

There is a third place in the netherworld, called the Lake of Fire, that is unoccupied at present. However, after Judgment Day, the condemned souls in *Gehenna* and the demons who had been in *Tartarus* (2 Peter 2:4), the demons who had been on earth, and Satan himself will all be cast into the Lake of Fire as the final judgment. This is the part that lasts forever.

✠ **Revelation 20:** ¹⁴ Then Death and Hades were thrown into the lake of fire. This is the second death, the lake of fire. ¹⁵ And if anyone's name was not found written in the book of life, he was thrown into the lake of fire.

✠ **Revelation 21:** ⁸ But as for the cowardly, the faithless, the detestable, as for murderers, the sexually immoral, sorcerers, idolaters, and all liars, their portion will be in the lake that burns with fire and sulfur, which is the second death.

THE LIVING DEAD: WHAT IS HELL LIKE?

Some view Hell as a customized torture suited for each person. But the nature of Hell is a universal standard that encapsulates the worst possible scenario. In answering the question any tourist would pose about their destination—what is Hell like?—here are some helpful, though distasteful expectations:

Hell Is Unbearably Hot

This description has become proverbial to us. In South Africa there is literally a town called Hot-as-Hell, situated in an arid desert region known for its unrelenting dry heat. The flames of Hell are not just the stuff of comic strips and descriptions from Dante's *Inferno*—the fiery heat is the most common characteristic used by biblical authors.

- **Matthew 13:** [41] The Son of Man will send his angels, and they will gather out of his kingdom all causes of sin and all law-breakers, [42] and throw them into the fiery furnace. In that place there will be weeping and gnashing of teeth.

- **Mark 9:** [43] And if your hand causes you to sin, cut it off. It is better for you to enter life crippled than with two hands to go to hell, to the unquenchable fire.

- **Luke 3:** [17] His winnowing fork is in his hand, to clear his threshing floor and to gather the wheat into his barn, but the chaff he will burn with unquenchable fire.

- **Jude:** ...[7] just as Sodom and Gomorrah and the surrounding cities, which likewise indulged in sexual immorality and pursued unnatural desire, serve as an example by undergoing a punishment of eternal fire.

- **Revelation 21:** [8] But as for the cowardly, the faithless, the detestable, as for murderers, the sexually immoral, sorcerers, idolaters, and all liars, their portion will be in the lake that burns with fire and sulfur, which is the second death.

I have heard of a planet that was recently discovered that is incredibly hot and simultaneously stormy. Astronomers surmise that the temperature on that orb is consistently over 3,000 degrees Fahrenheit and that sand storms from massive blasts of wind would turn the sand into sheets of glass. Imagine having a body that was immortal, and thus could not be permanently injured by that climate. One would live out one's days in constant agony, and yet without the relief of death.

Hell Is Dark

One of the strange ironies of Hell is that although it is known for the flames that seem to be perpetually blazing, it is also depressingly dark.

+ **Matthew 8:** [11] I tell you, many will come from east and west and recline at table with Abraham, Isaac, and Jacob in the kingdom of heaven, [12] while the sons of the kingdom will be thrown into the outer darkness. In that place there will be weeping and gnashing of teeth. (Also see, Matthew 22:13; 25:30).

+ **Jude:** [6] And the angels who did not stay within their own position of authority, but left their proper dwelling, he has kept in eternal chains under gloomy darkness until the judgment of the great day—

Hell Is Physically Agonizing.

In Luke 16 the rich man is described as "being in torment" and says, "I am in agony." He is clearly experiencing unquenchable thirst and is desperate for even a momentary flicker of relief from a drop of water on his lips.

✢ **Matthew 24:** [50] The master of that servant will come on a day when he does not expect him and at an hour he does not know [51] and will cut him in pieces and put him with the hypocrites. In that place there will be weeping and gnashing of teeth.

Hell Is Psychologically Distressing

Remember how distressed the rich man is? The place is marked not only by physical torment but also by the psychological trauma of intense anxiety, frustration, and regret.

✢ **Matthew 8:** . . . [12] while the sons of the kingdom will be thrown into the outer darkness. In that place there will be weeping and gnashing of teeth.

The punishment involves being rejected by your Creator, which must be the most devastating emotional blow imaginable.

✢ **Matthew 7:** [22] On that day many will say to me, "Lord, Lord, did we not prophesy in your name, and cast out demons in your name, and do many mighty works in your name?" [23] And then will I declare to them, "I never knew you; depart from me, you workers of lawlessness."

✢ **Revelation 22:** [14] Blessed are those who wash their robes, so that they may have the right to the tree of life and that they may enter the city by the gates. [15] Outside are the dogs and sorcerers and the sexually immoral and murderers and idolaters, and everyone who loves and practices falsehood.

✦ NO EXIT: HELL IS FOREVER ✦

Another aspect of Hell that sets it apart from all other destinations, is that it is a sentence, not a spot for visitors. And the sentence is always the same: eternity.

✦ **Matthew 25:** [46] And these will go away into eternal punishment, but the righteous into eternal life.

✦ **Mark 9:** [47] And if your eye causes you to sin, tear it out. It is better for you to enter the kingdom of God with one eye than with two eyes to be thrown into hell, [48] "where their worm does not die and the fire is not quenched."

Notice that the duration of life in Heaven is identical to that of damnation in Hell: eternal. Scot McKnight's explanation is helpful:

✦✦✦

Because [the Greek word in the New Testament] *aionios* ("eternal") modifies both punishment and life in Matthew 25:46, it stands to reason that the same quality and temporal connotations are in view. That is to say, however long the life extends is how long the punishment lasts; the durations are identical.

✦✦✦

The apostles were just as clear about the length of the sentence, concurring with Jesus on this distressing detail:

✦ **Jude:** [6] And the angels who did not stay within their own position of authority, but left their proper dwelling, he has kept in eternal chains under gloomy darkness until the judgment of the great day— [7] just as Sodom and Gomorrah and the surrounding cities, which likewise indulged in sexual immorality and pursued unnatural desire, serve as an example by undergoing a punishment of eternal fire.

✦ **Revelation 14:** [11] And the smoke of their torment goes up forever and ever, and they have no rest, day or night, these worshipers of the beast and its image, and whoever receives the mark of its name.

✦ **Revelation 20:** ... [10] and the devil who had deceived them was thrown into the lake of fire and sulfur where the beast and the false prophet were, and they will be tormented day and night forever and ever.

Some may question the justice of an eternal sentence meted out for the sins committed in a single lifetime. Surely— as the argument goes—the sins of seventy years doesn't deserve punishment that goes on forever. But the theological reason is that sin is not punished according to its breadth but its depth. Put another way, it is not what sins you commit or how many you commit or for how long you commit them, but against whom you commit them.

A single sin against an infinitely holy God earns an infinite punishment. This is another problem with the idea that "really bad people" go to Hell, but "decent, law-abiding citizens" go to Heaven. No one is infinitely decent, and so all of us are in an equally damnable position before the infinitely holy God whom we have all offended to some degree.

If that scares you spitless, join the club. But take heart, good news about how to escape Hell is coming in Chapter 7.

DEATH BY DEGREES:
LEVELS OF PUNISHMENT IN HELL

Think about these clues regarding degrees of punishment.

- Judas is said to be in "his own place" (Acts 1:25), which has been interpreted by some as referring to a reserved spot in Hell.

- Pharisees's converts were said to be "twice the son of Hell" as their mentors (Matthew 23:15).

- And in Matthew 11:23–24 Jesus thundered, "And you, Capernaum, will you be exalted to heaven? You will be brought down to Hades. For if the mighty works done in you had been done in Sodom, it would have remained until this day. But I tell you that it will be more tolerable on the day of judgment for the land of Sodom than for you."

- In Luke 12:42–48 the parable lists as consequences two differing degrees of punishment for disobedience. For those who sinned without knowing they were doing wrong, the punishment was limited to only a "few blows," while those who rebelled wilfully were sentenced to receive "many blows." This indicates to us that Jesus recognized degrees of punishment, depending on how much a person knows about what he or she is doing.

Note that the degree of punishment is not based on how much sin you did or what kind of sin you committed, but the appraisal is based on how much truth had been revealed to you.

- Hebrews 10:29: How much worse punishment, do you think, will be deserved by the one who has spurned the Son of God, and has profaned the blood of the covenant by which he was sanctified, and has outraged the Spirit of grace?

That there are degrees of punishment in the afterlife is strongly implied in the teachings of Scripture. (For an in-depth discussion of the degrees of reward and forfeiture of reward for believers, see a little book my mom recommends called *The Preacher's Payday*, by yours truly).

In summary, it is accurate to think of Hell as a place with physical dimensions that can be experienced as a reality. But at the same time it is to be understood as a realm that is not rooted in the same space and time as our lives here on earth. It is a spiritual dimension. Just as Heaven has trees and rivers and creatures that eat and speak and walk, in the same way Hell is a place with a landscape and a climate and population. It is painfully hot, depressingly dark, and teeming with the living dead.

This raises the question of who or what will occupy Hell. No visitor's guide would be complete without a discussion of the population. Let's delve into demonic demographics and meet the inmates of Hell.

❖❖❖

The Gated Community: Hell's Population

In my freshman English literature class our assigned reading included the play *No Exit* by existentialist philosopher Jean-Paul Sartre. We could either read it or watch a performance staged by a freshman drama class. The performance option induced me to ask a cute co-ed lit major for a date. This, combined with the fact that I could eliminate a reading assignment in ninety minutes, made the choice easy.

All I had heard about the play was that it was "an interesting take on Hell." I pictured scary scenes that could potentially prompt my date to grip my flexed arm and allow me to console her. I was wrong.

The play was devoid of all fright, suspense, or action of any kind. The curtain lifts on three characters in a room who begin to chat for what feels like much more than ninety minutes. Then the curtain falls. That is the play. Twice I had to squeeze my date's arm to stop her snoring.

What you discover from the characters' dialogue is that they are all deceased people and that the cramped room they are in represents their eternal living quarters in the afterlife. They are not quite sure if this is meant to be Heaven or Hell. As the play progresses, the characters become bored by each other's company and begin to get snippy with one another.

The snide comments and irritation escalates until eventually they are all totally exasperated and desperately unhappy with each other. It is then that they realize they are not in Heaven—they are in Hell. And that is when a pensive character utters Sartre's immortal diagnosis of the human condition: "*L'enfer c'est les autres . . .*": Hell is other people.

Although my date would probably not have used the word "interesting" to describe the evening, the play *was* an interesting take on Hell. For me, it highlighted the reality that much of life on earth's unpleasantness—crime, war, divorce, abuse, rejection—is only present because of other people.

As we have seen, Hell in reality is far worse than what we could experience in this life. But Sartre did touch on one element of torment that the Bible also describes: the inhabitants of Hell.

✤ HELL'S ANGELS ✤

Demons don't hang out in Hell comparing pitchforks and sending Screwtape e-mails from the netherworld. Their preferred habitat is Planet Earth. Understandably, they don't particularly want to go to Hell. Remember the deviled ham in Luke 8?

✤✤✤

Luke 8: ³⁰ Jesus then asked him, "What is your name?" And he said, "Legion," for many demons had entered him. ³¹ And they begged him not to command them to depart into the abyss.

✤✤✤

These demons had been caught red-handed by the Son of God, whom they recognized immediately. Incidentally, this account shows that these spiritual beings can possess a human body and, furthermore, that multiple demons can reside in the same physical space. We also learn from what followed that demons can possess animals (pigs in this case).

Seeing Jesus struck a chord of fear in these demons that almost makes you feel sorry for them! They are terrified of Jesus because he possesses the authority to instantaneously sentence them to a premature incarceration in the dreaded abyss. This is their worst nightmare. So much for the idea that demons are natives of Hell. They view Hell as a prison to be avoided at all costs.

In Daniel 10, demons are described as having authority over particular geographic locations and are even named for the region they oversee. For example, the "Prince of Persia [Iraq]" and "Prince of Greece" are identified as individual demons.

So, demons do not live in Hell, at least not by choice. But they will become inmates of that prison in the future. They seem aware of this, as evidenced by their terrified question:

✤✤✤✤

Matthew 8: ²⁹ And behold, they cried out, "What have you to do with us, O Son of God? Have you come here to torment us before the time?"

✤✤✤✤

But there are some hapless demons who have already met their eternal fate and are no longer permitted to roam freely on earth.

✤✤✤✤

2 Peter 2: ⁴ For if God did not spare angels [fallen angels or demons] when they sinned, but cast them into hell [*Tartarus*] and committed them to chains of gloomy darkness to be kept until the judgment . . . . [See also, Jude 6 and Genesis 6 for hints as to who these demons might be.]

✤✤✤✤

To clarify, demons are mostly located on earth, in a spiritual form, but they are also able to possess physical bodies. Their future fate is to be locked into the abyss, which eventually will be thrown into the Lake of Fire. Currently there are a few demons who have been incarcerated prematurely in the abyss. It is reasonable to assume that when people's souls are condemned to Hell they will not encounter many demons immediately, but eventually their fate will be the same as all creatures who are forbidden to enter Heaven: the Lake of Fire.

THE DEVIL'S IN THE DETAILS: WHERE SATAN DWELLS

As with demons, it is a misconception to assume that Satan currently dwells in Hell.

✦✦✦✦

Job 1: [6] Now there was a day when the sons of God came to present themselves before the Lord, and Satan also came among them. [7] The Lord said to Satan, "From where have you come?" Satan answered the Lord and said, "From going to and fro on the earth, and from walking up and down on it."

✦✦✦✦

Satan inhabits the earth, just like the other fallen angels. But the destiny of Satan is predicted in some startling detail throughout the Bible:

✦✦✦✦

Revelation 20: [1] Then I saw an angel coming down from heaven, holding in his hand the key to the bottomless pit and a great chain. [2] And he seized the dragon, that ancient serpent, who is the devil and Satan, and bound him for a thousand years, ... [7] And when the thousand years are ended, Satan will be released from his prison [8] and will come out to deceive the nations that are at the four corners of the earth, Gog and Magog, to gather them for battle; their number is like the sand of the sea. [9] And they marched up over the broad plain of the earth and surrounded the camp of the saints and the beloved city, but fire came down from heaven and consumed them, [10] and the devil who had deceived them was thrown into the lake of fire and sulfur where the beast and the false prophet were, and they will be tormented day and night forever and ever.

⁜⁜⁜⁜

There is a fascinating prophecy in the Book of Isaiah. It is difficult to interpret, but most commentators agree that the prophecy is describing the fall of Satan from Heaven, and his doom in Hell.

⁜⁜⁜⁜

Isaiah 14: [9] Sheol [Hell] beneath is stirred up to meet you when you come; it rouses the shades to greet you, all who were leaders of the earth; it raises from their thrones all who were kings of the nations. [10] All of them will answer and say to you: "You too have become as weak as we! You have become like us!" [11] Your pomp is brought down to Sheol, the sound of your harps; maggots are laid as a bed beneath you, and worms are your covers. [12] How you are fallen from heaven, O Day Star, son of Dawn! How you are cut down to the ground, you who laid the nations low! [13] You said in your heart, "I will ascend to heaven; above the stars of God I will set my throne on high; I will sit on the mount of assembly in the far reaches of the north; [14] I will ascend above the heights of the clouds; I will make myself like the Most High." [15] But you are brought down to Sheol, to the far reaches of the pit.

✦✦✦✦

This prophecy appears to be referring to Satan when he was an angel in Heaven. He decided in his heart to usurp God's throne. Having never witnessed any sin, rebellion, or disobedience, the angels had no concept of God's power, holiness, and justice. I think Satan actually thought he could take God! Anyway, things did not turn out well for Satan and the angels he managed to dupe into joining his coup. Satan was cast out of Heaven and will eventually be dragged down to Hell, where the souls of the damned will taunt him.

✦ WHO'S THE BOSS? ✦

Some view Satan as the manager, CEO, or ruler of hell. For example, scholar John Gerstner says, "Hell is where Satan rules."

But Satan is not the captain of Hell, is on earth at present, and will eventually be a captive, just like everyone else who is there. You may have a question about whether there is anyone "in charge." If it's not Satan, then who rules Hell? The answer might catch you by surprise, but the Bible says unequivocally that the one who rules over Hell is God himself.

Since God is omnipresent, his ontological presence in Hell is expected. The Bible shows God as being able to manifest his presence in various ways (for example, in the burning bush of Exodus 4, the glory resting on the Ark of the Covenant, as well as in the person of Jesus Christ). The way his presence is manifest in Hell is in the power of his judgment.

As scholar Robert Peterson explains in his seminal theological work on eternal punishment,

We need to reconsider the notion that God is absent from hell. In one sense he *is* absent from hell. This is why Paul says that unbelievers "will be shut out from the presence of the Lord" (2 Thessalonians 1:9). God is not present in hell in grace and blessing. However, since God is everywhere present, he is present in hell. Although he is not there in grace and blessing, he is there in holiness and wrath. We read in Revelation 14:10 that the unsaved will "drink of the wine of God's fury" and "be tormented with burning sulfur in the presence . . . of the Lamb." The world *Lamb* occurs twenty-eight times in the book of Revelation, and every occurrence except one (13:11) is a symbol for Christ. The wicked will suffer eternally in Christ's holy presence!

The New Testament is clear on the fact that God rules Hell.

- ✣ **Matthew 10:** [28] And do not fear those who kill the body but cannot kill the soul. Rather fear him who can destroy both soul and body in hell.
- ✣ **Matthew 25:** [41] Then he will say to those on his left, "Depart from me, you cursed, into the eternal fire prepared for the devil and his angels."

In fact, Jesus claims to have the authority to judge people and sentence them to Hell.

❖❖❖❖

John 5: [25] "Truly, truly, I say to you, an hour is coming, and is now here, when the dead will hear the voice of the Son of God, and those who hear will live. [26] For as the Father has life in himself, so he has granted the Son also to have life in himself. [27] And he has given him authority to execute judgment, because he is the Son of Man. [28] Do not marvel at this, for an hour is coming when all who are in the tombs will hear his voice [29] and come out, those who have done good to the resurrection of life, and those who have done evil to the resurrection of judgment.

❖❖❖❖

THE DOMAIN OF THE DAMNED: WHERE THE UNRIGHTEOUS SPEND ETERNITY

Who are the people who end up in Hell? Paul describes them simply as "those who do not know God and do not obey the gospel of Jesus Christ" (2 Thessalonians 1:8). Jesus also disappointed those who thought they were "good enough" to go to Heaven because they trusted in their résumé of good deeds instead of a relationship of trust with the Savior. Jesus places a premium on their relationship with him, not a list of accomplishments.

❖❖❖❖

Matthew 7: [22] On that day many will say to me, "Lord, Lord, did we not prophesy in your name, and cast out demons in your name, and do many mighty works in your name?" [23] And then will I declare to them,

"I never knew you; depart from me, you workers of lawlessness."

✦✦✦

A lack of relationship with Jesus means that those people who are not forgiven for their sins are still labeled by them. And since their sins have not been wiped clean by the sacrifice of Jesus (as these people rejected him as their Lord and Savior) they are doomed to bear the guilt forever:

✦ **Matthew 13:** [41] The Son of Man will send his angels, and they will gather out of his kingdom all causes of sin and all law-breakers, [42] and throw them into the fiery furnace. In that place there will be weeping and gnashing of teeth.

✦ **Galatians 5:** [19] Now the works of the flesh are evident: sexual immorality, impurity, sensuality, [20] idolatry, sorcery, enmity, strife, jealousy, fits of anger, rivalries, dissensions, divisions, [21] envy, drunkenness, orgies, and things like these. I warn you, as I warned you before, that those who do such things will not inherit the kingdom of God.

✦ **Revelation 21:** [7] The one who conquers will have this heritage, and I will be his God and he will be my son. [8] But as for the cowardly, the faithless, the detestable, as for murderers, the sexually immoral, sorcerers, idolaters, and all liars, their portion will be in the lake that burns with fire and sulfur, which is the second death.

✦ **Revelation 22:** [14] Blessed are those who wash their robes, so that they may have the right to the tree of life and that they may enter the city by the gates. [15] Outside are the dogs [derogatory term for the irreligious] and sorcerers and the sexually immoral and murderers and idolaters, and everyone who loves and practices falsehood.

So . . . see you in Hell?

I experienced a heartbreaking moment in my relationship with a loved one when he dismissed my efforts to share my beliefs, saying, "I wouldn't want to be in Heaven anyway—all my friends will be in Hell." He went on to describe his vision of Hell as a place of hedonistic pleasure and partying, unrestrained by the strictures of religious morality. In effect, he was putting together a home-brewed concoction of what he thought Hell would be like, picking and choosing from religion while ignoring the parts that seemed less desirable to him.

In the parable of the rich man and Lazarus, Jesus depicts a scene where the occupant of Hell is able to interact with Abraham, but not Lazarus. Interestingly, although the heavenly occupants are named, the rich man is conspicuously nameless. Is it possible Jesus was hinting at the anonymity that comes from being stripped of one's identity?

There seems to be a notion among some that Hell is a place that is much like earth, only without the judgment of overbearing pious people. I've met people who think of the afterlife as one unending party where inhibitions are cast off forever and there is no morality, conscience, or law enforcement. People who hate God's rules want to experience a life without them. That is understandable. But what they don't realize is how much grace and goodness those rules bring to life. Theologians call this "common grace" in that it is common to all mankind. Without it, existence is a very poor state indeed.

Jesus spoke of common grace this way:

✤✤✤✤

Matthew 5: [44] But I say to you, Love your enemies and pray for those who persecute you, [45] so that you may be sons of your Father who is in heaven. For he makes his sun rise on the evil and on the good, and sends rain on the just and on the unjust.

✤✤✤✤

And God is said to be the source of all goodness in this life. Everything that is enjoyable or pleasant or wholesome is a gift from him.

✤✤✤✤

James 1: [17] Every good gift and every perfect gift is from above, coming down from the Father of lights with whom there is no variation or shadow due to change.

✤✤✤✤

Part of God's good gift to earth is government and authorities that enforce justice.

✤✤✤✤

Romans 13: [17] Let every person be subject to the governing authorities. For there is no authority except from God, and those that exist have been instituted by God.

✤✤✤✤

Another gift common to all societies is the gift of marriage, which God calls the "grace of life" (1 Peter 3:7).

Being in Hell is not only an escape from God's rules, but

it is a rejection of His grace. Imagine a world where nothing good ever happens and nothing enjoyable is ever experienced: no mercy, no gifts, no pleasantness. Far from a wild party, Hell as a rejection of common grace is a pitiless, mirthless place. That is what Hell is like. So much for hedonism.

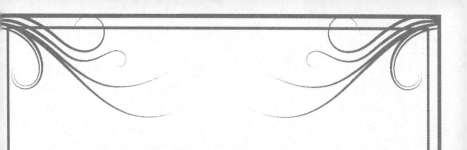

chapter

6

❖❖❖❖

Dead-End Streets:
How to Go to Hell

Brian Clark worked for Euro Bankers in the South Tower of the World Trade Center in New York City. On September 11, 2001, the fire alarm sounded seconds after the North Tower was struck by an airplane. Clark and his colleagues were reassured by a voice over the public address system that said, "Building Two is secure. There is no need to evacuate Building Two." Moments later, at 9:03 a.m., Building Two was struck by the second plane.

Clark was on the eighty-fourth floor, only three floors above the collision. His colleagues left their offices and filtered into the three emergency stairwells. Clark randomly chose stairwell A to make his exit.

At that time, the evacuees had no idea how much danger they were in. No one knew this was an orchestrated terrorist attack that would shortly level both towers, killing thousands.

As Clark began his descent, a group of people met him on their way up to the roof. They insisted that the stairwell below was blocked by debris and was impassable. This group encouraged everyone they encountered to follow them up to the perceived safety of the rooftop. While the argument ensued, Clark heard a cry for help. He left the discussion in order to locate the voice. He found Stanley Praimnath trapped in an office on the eighty-first floor where the plane's wing had lodged. Clark helped him escape. Praimnath hugged and kissed his rescuer and the two entered stairwell A. By now everyone else had gone to the roof. Clark and Praimnath worked together to clear the blockage in the staircase and they slowly descended stairwell A.

Only two others who had been above where the plane had struck used that escape route. Everyone else either remained in their offices, or tried the other stairwells, or waited on the roof. And they all died.

This remarkable account is a poignant reminder that there are situations in life in which choices we make have very different outcomes. And as with the victims of the senseless, inhuman evil who died in the World Trade Center, we often we have no idea if the way we have chosen will lead to escape or danger.

Every day approximately 154,000 people leave this life and enter into eternity. That's three every second. About 3,000 will die while you are reading this chapter, which is approximately the same number of lives lost in the tragedy of 9/11.

How many of these souls will go to Hell? In the Bible, the prognosis is that many will.

After hearing Jesus preach, his disciples asked him:

Luke 13: [23] And someone said to him, "Lord, will those who are saved be few?" And he said to them, [24] "Strive to enter through the narrow door. For many, I tell you, will seek to enter and will not be able."

On another occasion, when the disciples heard how impossible the standard for entry to Heaven is, they said:

Luke 18: [26] . . . "Then who can be saved?" [27] But he [Jesus] said, "What is impossible with men is possible with God."

The paucity of survivors is a disturbing motif in the New Testament:

✢ **Matthew 7:** ¹³ Enter by the narrow gate. For the gate is wide and the way is easy that leads to destruction, and those who enter by it are many. ¹⁴ For the gate is narrow and the way is hard that leads to life, and those who find it are few.

✢ **Matthew 7:** ²² On that day many will say to me, "Lord, Lord, did we not prophesy in your name, and cast out demons in your name, and do many mighty works in your name?" ²³ And then will I declare to them, "I never knew you; depart from me, you workers of lawlessness."

✢ **Matthew 22:** ¹⁴ For many are called, but few are chosen.

✢ **Philippians 3:** ¹⁸ For many, of whom I have often told you and now tell you even with tears, walk as enemies of the cross of Christ. ¹⁹ Their end is destruction, their god is their belly, and they glory in their shame, with minds set on earthly things.

✢ **1 Corinthians 6:** ⁹ Or do you not know that the unrighteous will not inherit the kingdom of God? Do not be deceived: neither the sexually immoral, nor idolaters, nor adulterers, nor men who practice homosexuality, ¹⁰ nor thieves, nor the greedy, nor drunkards, nor revilers, nor swindlers will inherit the kingdom of God.

✢ **2 Peter 2:** ² And many will follow their sensuality, and because of them the way of truth will be blasphemed.

The chilling reality according to the Bible is that it is exceedingly easy to go to Hell. Most people end up there, while only a few escape.

One way to get there is simply to do nothing. We are all born with a default setting bound for Hell. We all live in a burning building. There are many ways labeled "escape" but most of those routes are dead ends. If you take no action and do nothing, you are doomed; if you take the wrong way out, you will get stuck; if you look for rescue in the wrong place, you will be disappointed. The Bible identifies the dead ends and warns us to avoid them.

There are three widely held beliefs that people assume are escape routes to avoid Hell: associating with the "right" religion, waiting for proof, and trusting in your own goodness. According to the Bible, each is a deadly cul-de-sac of false hope.

DEAD-END ESCAPE ROUTE #1: RELYING ON THE "RIGHT" RELIGION

To which religion did the rich man subscribe? He was not a heathen unbeliever or pagan pantheist. Nor was he an atheist who denied the existence of God. He was a man who called Abraham "Father," and who Abraham in turn acknowledged as "my child." In other words, he was a Jew.

✤✤✤

Luke 16: [24] And he called out, "Father Abraham, have mercy on me, . . ." [25] But Abraham said, "Child, . . ."

✤✤✤

The rich man calls Abraham "Father," and Abraham acknowledges him as "Child."

This is very significant. Jesus is signaling to his audience that the rich man was not a pagan Gentile—he was a Jew, like Jesus was at the time, and like his intended audience would have been. The rich man was not some Ammonite, Moabite, Perrezzite, or other Canaanite nonbeliever. He wasn't a Greek pantheist or a demonic Satanist. He was as Jewish as Jesus. He was a descendant of Abraham. He had the "right" religion.

Remember that when Jesus was telling this parable, the only religion God considered acceptable was Judaism. The Old Testament was the whole Bible for them. It was the Old Testament prophets who had revealed the way of salvation to the Jews. And it was through the Jews that salvation was made available to all other nations. From the time that God called Abraham to be the father of the Jewish nation, if you wanted to be saved from your sins, you had to become Jewish. You had to adopt their system—the only acceptable way of atoning for your sins. You had to keep the Law of Moses, all 613 rules and regulations. You had to keep the feasts and become Jewish in every way. You had to move to Israel or at least visit Jerusalem annually.

One example is the Gentile Moabite Ruth, who married a Jew and chose to renounce her idolatry and become Jewish. Conversion was a three-step process. You had to sacrifice a lamb, take a ceremonial bath, and, if you were male, get circumcised. Needless to say, Gentile conversion was not a common occurrence in the ancient Near East!

Most Jews were Jewish because they were born into a Jewish home. The majority of Jews were not people who had independently chosen to renounce their Gentile ways and convert. Most Jews were simply raised as Jews. This led to some Jews just going through the motions and practicing the sacrifices and prayers as if they were merely part of their cultural traditions. Many today, no matter what their religion, also unthinkingly practice the traditions they were handed without appropriating the meaning for themselves.

But, according to the Bible, just being born into the right religion by birth cannot save you. (I was born in a hospital; that doesn't make me a doctor.) Remember John the Baptist? In Luke 3:8 he warned those who were ethnically and culturally

Jewish: "Bear fruits in keeping with repentance. And do not begin to say to yourselves, 'We have Abraham as our father.' For I tell you, God is able from these stones to raise up children for Abraham."

Whatever your religion, it is not the deciding factor as to whether you escape Hell or not. This is a false assurance of many who were born into a Christian home or were baptized as infants, plod through the motions of Sunday School class, communion, youth group, serving in the church, and even giving money to the ministry—only to grow up and leave the church and its teachings as soon as they are old enough to drive. Or, equally as bad, to simply go through the motions.

DEAD-END ESCAPE ROUTE #2: WAITING FOR PROOF

There are people who view religion quite passively. They carry on with their lives, assuming that if God wants to get their attention, it is up to Him to do it effectively enough so that they don't have to put any effort in. It's an attitude of "If God wants me to believe in him, then he needs to prove to me that he exists." They are oblivious of the commands God has issued to them in his word. For example:

+ **Isaiah 55:** [6] "Seek the Lord while he may be found; call upon him while he is near; [7] let the wicked forsake his way, and the unrighteous man his thoughts; let him return to the Lord, that he may have compassion on him, and to our God, for he will abundantly pardon.

+ **Acts 17:** [30] The times of ignorance God overlooked, but now he commands all people everywhere to repent, [31] because he has fixed a day on which he will judge the world in righteousness by a man whom he has appointed; and of this he has given assurance to all by raising him from the dead."

The rich man begged Abraham to send Lazarus to warn his brothers of Hell.

⁘⁘⁘

Luke 16: ²⁷And he said, "Then I beg you, father, to send him to my father's house— ²⁸ for I have five brothers— so that he may warn them, lest they also come into this place of torment . . . ." ³⁰ And he said, "No, father Abraham, but if someone goes to them from the dead, they will repent."

⁘⁘⁘

The rich man wrongly thinks that his brothers (and by implication himself) have lacked the necessary information for salvation. He avers that if a dead man comes back from the afterlife to warn them, then they will believe. Incidentally, this particular proof was furnished to humanity by God on a number of occasions, but has been rejected by many. Indeed, what sets Christianity apart from other faiths is the belief that Jesus rose from the dead.

The eyewitness reports of Christ's resurrection contained in the New Testament form the essence of the Christian faith. In addition to his own resurrection, before Jesus was crucified he miraculously raised a man from the dead as proof of his identity. I find it ironic that the man in this story was a man named . . . wait for it . . . Lazarus (see John 11). After Lazarus of Bethany rose from the dead, the event was reported to some religious leaders who responded by plotting to assassinate Jesus.

In the parable of the rich man and Lazarus, the words of Abraham seem harsh, but they are precisely accurate.

Luke 16: ²⁹ But Abraham said, "They have Moses and the Prophets; let them hear them." ³⁰ And he said, "No, father Abraham, but if someone goes to them from the dead, they will repent." ³¹ He said to him, "If they do not hear Moses and the Prophets, neither will they be convinced if someone should rise from the dead."

People wrongly think that it is God's job to provide proof of His existence that meets with their standard of approval. But possessing evidence is no guarantee of an escape from Hell. It is what one does with the proof.

Matthew 7: ²¹ "Not everyone who says to me, 'Lord, Lord,' will enter the kingdom of heaven, but the one who does the will of my Father who is in heaven. ²² On that day many will say to me, 'Lord, Lord, did we not prophesy in your name, and cast out demons in your name, and do many mighty works in your name?' ²³ And then will I declare to them, 'I never knew you; depart from me, you workers of lawlessness.'"

Here are people who believe they have experienced miracles, in fact performed miracles. But they had no relationship with Jesus and were therefore not permitted into his kingdom.

Believing that Jesus existed and was powerful enough to

do miracles is not enough to save you. Even demons believe in the truth of Jesus's miracles. Faith is empty if it is not a personal apprehension of truth with an application to one's own life.

> ✛ **James 2:** [18] But someone will say, "You have faith and I have works." Show me your faith apart from your works, and I will show you my faith by my works. [19] You believe that God is one; you do well. Even the demons believe— and shudder! [20] Do you want to be shown, you foolish person, that faith apart from works is useless?

> ✛ **2 Corinthians 5:** . . . [7] for we walk by faith, not by sight.

Faith means trusting what God says because you believe His word, not because you see proof.

Implicit in the rich man's reasoning is an excuse for his own damnation: "Abraham, if I had seen a resurrection miracle, I would have believed. I am in Hell because God did not furnish me with enough proof of what He said."

What's Abraham's response? In Luke 16, verse 29 he says, "They have Moses and the Prophets; let them hear them . . . ;" in 31 he said to him, "If they do not hear Moses and the Prophets, neither will they be convinced if someone should rise from the dead."

In other words, Abraham says they do have enough proof. They have the Bible. Actually, they have what we call the Old Testament (what they knew as the *Tanak*), and that is all they need.

God has already supplied enough proof to authenticate his messengers. What saves you is believing in what the messengers say!

I know by this point you might be getting impatient for some conclusive guidance about what to do once you're *in* Hell. In this chapter, we learned about good ways to get to Hell, presumably so you can make plans to avoid doing those things. In summary:

To get to Hell,

a) do nothing; since people are born in sin, doing nothing about your salvation is to be condemned for your sin. Doing nothing will inevitably lead you to Hell.

b) do a mediocre job—in other words be "good enough." Since there are so many erroneously marked paths to "Heaven," it's pretty easy to end up in Hell just by doing what you hope is right. You might be relying on having the "right" religion, more or less avoiding a wicked lifestyle, and believing generally that Jesus exists.

c) believe in a way to salvation that is not acceptable to God, the Judge.

Think of all the options passengers of the *Titanic* had in terms of dying. They could do nothing and allow themselves to go down with the sinking ship. They could jump overboard and be sucked under when the ship went down. They could tread water and freeze to death. The paths to death were varied and numerous. But there was only one way to survive: to be rescued. There was no hope of swimming back to land. Their only hope was being pulled into one of the scarce lifeboats. In the same way, the paths that lead to Hell are innumerable, but the only way to salvation is a powerful, death-conquering Savior to rescue you.

Most people take assurance from the simple gamble that they are "good enough" and that their good works and intentions outweigh their sins. The sad reality is that the Bible says no one is "good enough."

DEAD-END ESCAPE ROUTE #3: BEING GOOD ENOUGH

Larry King is a formidable and entertaining interviewer. He has a knack for sparking discussions about what people want to hear. In

2005 he hosted a discussion on his *Larry King Live* TV show titled "What Happens After We Die?" The panel consisted of six well-known personalities who were considered experts on the topic.

The representatives were:

- Dr. John MacArthur, best-selling evangelical author, pastor, and theologian
- Father Michael Manning, a Roman Catholic priest and host of an international radio program
- Dr. Mahar Hathout, a physician and advisor to the Muslim Public Affairs Council
- Rabbi Marvin Hier, founder of the Simon Wiesenthal Center
- Ms. Ellen Johnson, the president of American Atheists
- Ms. Mary Ann Williamson, an author and lecturer on esoteric spirituality

These speakers represented disparate views, but they all strived admirably to maintain decorum and to be agreeable in their disagreement. There was, however, a moment when Larry had to wrangle his guests to make them move past a particular point of conflict. His lighthearted charm served to diffuse a potentially explosive moment, but the interaction is illuminating when it comes to the many different opinions people have about the best ways to avoid Hell. Here is an edited excerpt of a transcript.

The rabbi postulates that a person who does good deeds will go to Heaven. Note how the evangelical Christian pastor's contrary view is continually misunderstood by the atheist, the rabbi, and the interviewer; their preconceived misconceptions of the Christian view contorts their perception of what is being said:

LARRY KING: It's going to happen to everybody [i.e. death]. And we all wonder about it. When will it happen; what will it be like? And, of course, what happens after? We're going to try to piece together those questions tonight, especially with death so much in the news. . . . So we'll start with John MacArthur and the opinion of each of them, representing their own opinions or their faiths. John MacArthur, what happens had you die?

MACARTHUR: Well, when you die, you go to one of two places. According to scripture. You go out of the presence of God forever, or you go into the presence of God forever.

KING: Depending?

MACARTHUR: Depending upon your personal relationship with Jesus Christ, which is according to the Bible the only way to enter heaven.

KING: So therefore a Jew or a Muslim or a Buddhist will not go to heaven?

MACARTHUR: Christian theology and the scripture says that only through faith in Jesus Christ.

. . .

KING: Rabbi Hier, what will happen when you die?

HIER: . . . God never destroyed the Garden of Eden, and he held up the hope that people who *live righteously, with righteous conduct*, go to the eternal world, the world of the soul. And admission to that world is *based on righteous conduct and not based on any specific religion*. A righteous person of any religion and a *righteous person* who may, in the fact, be irreligious—

KING: [Interrupting] You mean atheist?

HIER: —would be granted because it is *determined by deeds*.

. . .

ELLEN JOHNSON: [In response to MacArthur] The price for eternal life and life after death is *obedience to church doctrine*? So you must *live a certain life* in preparation for that life after death? That I totally reject. I am not going to . . .

MACARTHUR: [Interrupting] So do I.

[CROSSTALK]

KING: Hold it, hold it, Ellen. [To MacArthur] you said you have to believe in Christ.

MACARTHUR: Well, yes . . . and at this point I respectfully disagree with the rabbi: *nobody can live a righteous life*. The Bible says that no one can obey the law of God. No one.

KING: So no one is going to heaven?

MACARTHUR: So no one can go to heaven on their own merits or on their own works. I don't care how many good works they do. The New Testament is crystal clear on the fact.

KING: So a *bad guy* who believes in Christ, he's going to heaven, and the *good guy* who doesn't is going to hell. That don't sound just.

. . .

MACARTHUR: No. It [God's justice] sends everybody to hell. We need grace. We need forgiveness. We need mercy. Only those who ask . . .

HIER: . . . When you take an exam, not everybody has to get 100. It's preposterous to think that when you say "righteous conduct" you mean perfect specimens. Human beings are not perfect specimens. In God's world, they will be accepted to eternity or eternal heaven *if they pass the exam*. What's a passing grade in heaven? I don't know. Maybe 67 and not 65. But the fact of the matter is if you—if you live the *decent life that is credible*, you *don't have to be perfect*.

KING: Let me get a break and come right back. I hope it's 51. We'll be right back. . . .

I love Larry's candor. Personally, I'd prefer the passing grade for Heaven to be even lower than 51. I wouldn't want to risk my eternity on the hope that my good works outweigh my sins, especially when you define a sin the way God does: every thought, word, and deed that falls short of God's standard!

This is one of the most common misconceptions about Heaven and Hell: the way to avoid Hell is to be "good enough."

Jesus didn't paint the rich man as being particularly wicked. If he had been malicious and brutal with Lazarus, then the point Jesus was making in his story wouldn't make sense. His whole premise is that we expect the rich man to be in Heaven, but we are surprised to find him in Hell.

This was the fallacy Dr. MacArthur was addressing in the *Larry King Live* interview. The rabbi opined that since nobody's perfect, the passing grade for Heaven must be lower than 100 percent. He guessed, a bit tongue-in-cheek, that it was in the sixtieth percentile range.

I'm with Larry, who facetiously added, "I hope it's 51." In fact, I would prefer the passing grade to be as low as possible; this is my eternal destiny after all.

But being good to Lazarus would not have made a saving difference in the life of the rich man. Paul said that salvation was "not a result of works, so that no one may boast" (Ephesians 2:9).

By the way, Father Abraham, who we find made it amply into Heaven, was not granted entrance due to his good works. His "good works" were imbued with flecks of tarnish too. For example, he lied repeatedly about Sarah being his sister so that she would get raped instead of him being killed. Oh, and he had a love child with a servant girl, and then to keep Sarah happy, he disowned her and the boy, Ishmael, which could arguably be deemed the beginning of the interminable Arab-Israeli conflict that rages to this day. Abraham was not commended by God for his good deeds, but for his faith.

Romans 4: [2] For if Abraham was justified by works, he has something to boast about, but not before God. [3] For

what does the Scripture say? "Abraham believed God, and it was counted to him as righteousness."

✦✦✦✦

It would be nice if the rabbi were right—that being relatively righteous compared to really bad guys suffices to secure us a passing grade. But the rabbi's opinion is the exact opposite of what the Bible teaches. God *does* expect perfection, and the pass mark *is* 100 percent.

✦ **Matthew 8:** [48] You therefore must be perfect, as your heavenly Father is perfect.

✦ **James 2:** [10] For whoever keeps the whole law but fails in one point has become accountable for all of it.

The Bible does agree with the rabbi on one point though: nobody attains that standard of perfection.

✦ **Romans 3:** . . . [10] as it is written: "None is righteous, no, not one;

✦ **Romans 3:** . . . [23] for all have sinned and fall short of the glory of God,

✦ **1 Kings 8:** [46] "If they sin against you—for there is no one who does not sin—and you are angry with them and give them to an enemy, so that they are carried away captive to the land of the enemy, far off or near,

✦ **Ecclesiastes 7:** [20] Surely there is not a righteous man on earth who does good and never sins.

Yikes. The bad news is that everybody deserves Hell. The pass mark for Heaven is 100, and no one can possibly attain a perfect score. So, who then goes to Heaven? If you ask that, then it means you are starting to understand the gospel.

Remember what Ms. Johnson, the president of the American Atheist society, said in the interview with Larry King?

ELLEN JOHNSON: [In response to MacArthur] The price for eternal life and life after death is *obedience to church doctrine*? So you must *live a certain life* in preparation for that life after death? That I totally reject. I am not going to . . .

MACARTHUR: [Interrupting] So do I.

The pastor agrees with the atheist! She has misunderstood what MacArthur said when he articulated the Christian view that people go to Heaven or Hell depending on their relationship to Jesus Christ (a relationship of faith and trust or a rejection of his sacrifice). Larry King then tries to clarify:

KING: Hold it, hold it, Ellen. [To MacArthur] you said you have to believe in Christ.

MACARTHUR: Well, yes . . . and at this point I respectfully disagree with the rabbi: *nobody can live a righteous life*. The Bible says that no one can obey the law of God. No one.

KING: So no one is going to heaven?

MACARTHUR: So no one can go to heaven on their own merits or on their own works.

It is amazing to me how many people think that the Bible teaches that the way to be saved is to be good or to do good. One of the clearest teachings of the Bible is that no one is good enough, no good deeds can pay back bad deeds, and that no one is saved by being good. The Bible says the way we are rescued from our guilt is by grace (a free gift of God) that was not earned by us but was earned by Jesus and given to us for free.

If one accepts this teaching of substitution, then the only part left to play is to trust in him as our Savior, and then his perfect life gets accredited to our accounts. Is this fair? No, it's called *grace*.

And it is why God is worthy of thanks, and praise, and worship. Here are some verses that make this abundantly clear:

+ **Ephesians 2:** [8] For by grace you have been saved through faith. And this is not your own doing; it is the gift of God, [9] not a result of works, so that no one may boast. [10] For we are his workmanship, created in Christ Jesus for good works, which God prepared beforehand, that we should walk in them.

+ **Galatians 2:** ... [16] yet we know that a person is not justified [made right with God, that is, forgiven] by works of the law but through faith in Jesus Christ, so we also have believed in Christ Jesus, in order to be justified by faith in Christ and not by works of the law, because by works of the law no one will be justified.

+ **2 Timothy 1:** [8] Therefore do not be ashamed of the testimony about our Lord, nor of me his prisoner, but share in suffering for the gospel by the power of God, [9] who saved us and called us to a holy calling, not because of our works but because of his own purpose and grace, which he gave us in Christ Jesus before the ages began,

+ **Romans 3:** [28] For we hold that one is justified by faith apart from works of the law.

After 9/11, Stanley Praimnath was interviewed about his recollections of his escape from the South Tower. A fascinating detail was that he and Brian Clark had felt no sense of urgency about their escape. They were taking their sweet time with the tiring descent. They took a brief break at the forty-fourth floor to talk with someone helping an injured person. When they got to the thirty-seventh floor, they took another rest. Both of them popped into offices and made personal phone calls to family, assuring them that they were not in any danger. Clark then called 911 and for three minutes calmly explained what they had experienced and where the emergency workers should go.

When they finally exited the building, rescue workers were yelling at them to run for their lives. Praimnath remarked to Clark that the buildings might collapse, but Clarke assured him that was impossible because of how solid the construction was. While he was still uttering that sentence, the South Tower collapsed right in front of them, a mere five minutes after they left the building.

Many people who are familiar with the Bible have a vague sense that Heaven and Hell must be real. But some people are perilously unaware of the urgency with which they should be considering these issues. They are either doing nothing to escape Hell, or randomly selecting an escape route that may or may not be effective. And still others are blissfully unaware that God has, before the creation of the world, been staging the most dramatic and widespread rescue operation in history, on their behalf. It is to the mechanics of this great escape we now turn our attention.

chapter

7

❖❖❖

The Great Escape:
Rescued from Hell

One balmy summer day in 1997, a fifty-seven-year-old Oklahoma woman named Rita Rupp was enjoying a leisurely road trip with her husband Floyd, sixty-seven. For no reason in particular, she began to fear that they might be in danger. She thought, "What if someone hijacks our car and kidnaps us? No one would even realize we're missing for days, and no one would come looking for us." So she hatched a plan.

Rita wrote a note, just in case she got kidnapped. She scrawled the note in appropriately distressed handwriting, "Help I've been kidnapped. Call the Highway Patrol." She also supplied her name and a helpful description of the van they were driving.

This eccentric emergency plan would actually have proven to be a pretty good idea in the event that at some point she had actually been kidnapped and managed to dispatch the note before being incapacitated.

The idea was rather harmless, albeit a bit quirky—except for one unforeseen eventuality. Mrs. Rupp's paranoia would have remained her private problem if on a bathroom break at a gas station the note hadn't inadvertently dropped out of her handbag. *Oops.*

A conscientious attendant found the alarming note and quickly notified the authorities, which then immediately issued alerts, mobilized patrol vehicles, and set up road blocks in four states.

All the while, Mr. and Mrs. Rupp were cruising along to their destination, blissfully unaware of the multiagency national rescue operation that been launched to save them.

Eventually, Mr. Rupp called his workplace to brag about the ocean view he was enjoying. His colleague responded, "You have no idea what's going on, do you?" Evidently he didn't. I wonder if this type of behavior from his dear wife was something he had grown accustomed to.

In the spiritual realm, many people, like the Rupps, are blissfully unaware of the epic rescue operation that has been underway on their behalf for millennia. They coast blithely through life without any idea of the sacrifice and planning that has been invested in their salvation.

In the previous chapter we looked at dead-end escape routes that people mistakenly take to avoid Hell. They trust in their family's inherited religion; they wait passively for God to furnish adequate proof of His existence. They work hard at being good, or at least good enough to counteract the bad, hoping to make a passing grade and go to Heaven.

But the New Testament explains that the way to avoid Hell is not by your efforts, but by a rescue, or salvation, plan that was undertaken by Jesus on your behalf. According to Scripture, your part is to believe. Your part is to trust in Jesus in a way that will slowly have an effect on your life. Your attitudes and actions will be altered by this faith, but the behavioral change is a *result* of your rescue; it is never done to earn salvation.

Think of yourself as living on a raft that is being pulled toward a deadly plunge down a steep waterfall. No matter what you do, it is not enough to escape the pull of the current. You can paddle with your efforts at good works. This makes you look like you are not drifting as fast as others. This might cause you to take comfort in knowing that you are doing better than many others who are making no effort at all.

Alternately, you may be one of the people waiting for proof that there is a deadly consequence coming. You see the signage that warns "Beware, danger ahead," but you feel that is not compelling enough evidence; those signs posts might just be the opinion of paranoid people.

Or, you might be someone who is distracted by your quest to make the raft comfortable. You work long hours, add to the menagerie of trinkets on your raft, and take great pride in how plush it is. You don't give much thought to the warning signs, and you even feel sorry for the people who are pitching their worldly goods overboard in order to try to paddle against the flow.

According to the Bible, Hell is the default destination for all people. So, how do we avoid that tragic end? The Bible maintains that we need rescue. This is where the concept of a Savior comes in. Obviously there are many theories on who the Savior is and how we can ask him to save us. But the New Testament proffers only one option. If you accept it as a reliable source of information on the afterlife and salvation, then decide for yourself what God says in his word, it is the only way to be saved:

✦ **John 14:** [6] Jesus said to him, "I am the way, and the truth, and the life. No one comes to the Father except through me. [7] If you had known me, you would have known my Father also. From now on you do know him and have seen him."

✦ **Acts 4:** [11] This Jesus is the stone that was rejected by you, the builders, which has become the cornerstone. [12] And there is salvation in no one else, for there is no other name under heaven given among men by which we must be saved."

✦ **Colossians 1:** [13] "He [God] has delivered us from the domain of darkness and transferred us to the kingdom of his beloved Son [Jesus], [14] in whom we have redemption, the forgiveness of sins."

✦ **Romans 5:** [6] "For while we were still weak, at the right time Christ died for the ungodly. . . . [9] Since, therefore, we have now been justified by his blood, much more shall we be saved by him from the wrath of God."

So how does salvation work in this context? How does faith apply the work of Christ to your life? The answer is found in one word: *substitution*.

✦ A SNEAKY SUBSTITUTION ✦

Charles Dickens is arguably one of the greatest storytellers of all time. At the climactic chapter of his epic masterpiece *A Tale of Two Cities*, Dickens provides a vivid illustration of the most significant theological concepts in the Bible: substitutionary rescue.

Charles Darnay and Sydney Carton are two men who are polar opposites of each other in many respects. Darnay is noble, honorable, and responsible. Carton, on the other hand, possesses none of these admirable qualities—and he knows it.

The fates of these antipodean characters are inextricably linked by two providential coincidences. First, they are both in love with the same woman, the enchanting Lucie Manette. And second, they happen to bear an uncanny physical resemblance to one another.

When Carton confesses to Lucie why he would never deserve her love, she can't help but agree with his assessment, and she marries Darnay. And though rebuffed by unrequited love, Carton declares in a moment of passion that he would "embrace any sacrifice for you and for those dear to you." This declaration proves to be prophetic when Carton is eventually faced with a unique opportunity to help his rival escape from prison.

Through a series of Dickensian twists and turns, Darnay ends up on death row in Paris, awaiting execution by guillotine. Carton secures a private visit with the prisoner where he drugs him, exchanges clothes with him, plants his own identification papers on him and calls to have the unconscious "visitor" removed from the jail cell. When Darnay awakes, he is a free man, and Carton bravely takes his place at the guillotine, all for the love of Lucie.

Though the illustration should not be pushed too far (in the novel it is the "bad" guy who redeems our opinion of him

None of this depends upon your contributions to the world, or your ability to live a "good" life. According to the Bible, you are like a drowning swimmer yanked from the sea by an able lifeguard. God planned the salvation, foreshadowed it, promised it, executed it, proved it, and declared it. All you have to do is believe Him. That is how you get the sacrifice of Jesus applied to your account. You get his righteousness, and he pays for your sin by his innocent blood on the cross. He bore the wrath on your behalf, and in return you get his perfect righteousness in your account, which makes you pass the 100 percent standard of perfection. It's called being justified—in other words, declared righteous by God.

Now, according to the Bible, does this mean that whoever believes in Jesus is perfect? Yes and no. If you've met Christians in your life, then you know that not all of them are perfect! When you place your trust in Jesus, God has declared you to be righteous, meaning that your guilt is forgiven and Jesus's actions have secured your salvation. However, the change in your attitudes, desires, and behavior in this life will take quite a bit longer to take root. It's called "sanctification," or the process of becoming more like Jesus in practice.

The Bible dictates that perfection cannot be attained in this life, but only in Heaven. This is what the Bible calls "glorification." It is the final step in your salvation: when you die, God makes you perfect in practice when you enter Heaven.

This should explain why Christians still sin. Everybody sins. But, if you are a Christian, hopefully once you are forgiven of your sin, you will begin to try to live like you know you should. The goal is to not to live in a moral way in order to earn your salvation, but in *response* to your salvation.

To understand sanctification, I am reminded of a Jewish fable of the boy who thought he was a rooster. This young lad refused to associate in a normal way with humans. He liked to scratch on the floor, peck at his food, and crow loudly at daybreak. And most disturbingly, he eschewed the use of clothing. This would be problematic for any family, but to compound the embarrassment, the boy just happened to be the eldest son of the king. This would-be fowl was the heir apparent to the royal throne. When diplomatic guests joined the royal family for a banquet, the king tried desperately to get the prince to dress and behave according to his position, but nothing could coax him out from under the table or get him to keep his clothes on.

Eventually a sage, an elderly advisor to the king, attempted something unconventional. He joined the boy under the table and also began to act like a rooster. After many days of roosterly behavior, the old man explained to the boy that although they were both roosters, there was no rule against a rooster wearing pants. The boy agreed and donned a pair of breeches.

The following day the old man said, "Although we are roosters, there is no shame in us wearing a shirt to match our trousers." The boy agreed. This occurred repeatedly over the next several days, and eventually they were both wearing a full suit of clothing, neatly groomed, and sitting at the king's table eating with utensils. Years later, when the prince was to be crowned king, the old wise man said to the boy, "We all know that you are a rooster at heart, but the country needs you to rule wisely. It's time to act like a king." The boy agreed.

To me this is a vivid picture of anyone who has been told what he or she is but still needs to grow into that position for himself or herself. For example, a sinner is declared righteous and told that he is the son of a King, namely God. But he still acts like an unreasoning animal at times. And yet, over the course of time, with wise guidance and much patience, one small degree at a time, we evolve in our behavior and attitudes, and we conform more and more to the standard Jesus already earned for us. It's what I call "becoming what you are in Christ."

✦ **Romans 8:** [29] For those whom he foreknew he also predestined to be conformed to the image of his Son, in order that he might be the firstborn among many brothers. [30] And those whom he predestined he also called, and those whom he called he also justified, and those whom he justified he also glorified.

✦ **2 Corinthians 3:** [18] And we all, with unveiled face, beholding the glory of the Lord, are being transformed into the same image from one degree of glory to another.

To summarize:

✦ The ways to Hell are myriad.

✦ The standard for Heaven is perfection.

✦ To Christians, nobody is perfectly righteous except Jesus Christ.

✦ According to the Bible, the only way to attain the 100 percent pass mark is for Jesus to take your sin and give you righteousness in a process of substitution.

✦ The Bible maintains that the only way to escape Hell is to be rescued.

On March 23, 2003, during Operation Iraqi Freedom, an American military convoy took a wrong turn and drove into an enemy ambush. Unable to adequately defend themselves, most of the unit was slaughtered. One unconscious nineteen-year-old soldier was taken prisoner in an Iraqi hospital, ominously named Saddam Hospital.

The soldier's name was PFC Jessica Lynch. This teenage girl was the first female American soldier ever to be taken as a prisoner of war.

For six days Lynch lay completely incapacitated with a broken thighbone, broken arm, and dislocated ankle. In her condition there was no chance of escape. A local doctor tried to help her by smuggling her to a U.S. checkpoint. But the guards at the checkpoint shot at the unidentified vehicle, preventing the delivery. Lynch was trapped behind enemy lines.

But her government was not idle. On April 1, an elite joint rescue squad consisting of Navy SEALs, Army Rangers, and other special forces, descended dramatically on Saddam Hospital alighting from helicopters. Taking no chances, they subdued every potential threat, including innocent doctors, nurses, and even other civilian patients!

Not realizing this massive onslaught was all being staged on her behalf, Jessica was fearful that the rescuers would leave her there or, worse, inadvertently shoot her. As the rescuers burst into Jessica's hospital room she cried out urgently, "I am an American soldier too!" The reassuring reply was, "We know, we're here for you," and a small cloth patch was pressed into her hand. It was an American flag. She was immediately whisked away by helicopter, and the rescue operation was not considered complete until she was delivered safely back to her family on American soil.

The Bible describes all humans as captives of sin. But the good news of the gospel is that Jesus Christ is our rescuer. God secured salvation for anyone who believes. He did this by sending His Son to live the perfect life on our behalf and die the death we deserve. We are all trapped behind enemy lines and doomed to an unthinkable end, but for anyone who is in Christ's spiritual kingdom, our rescue is guaranteed.

How do you avoid Hell? You can't. But God can rescue you, if you believe in His Son, Jesus Christ.

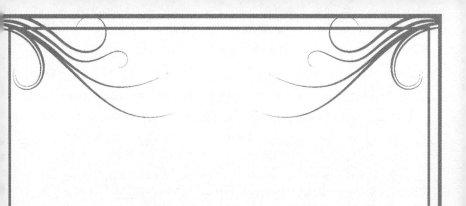

chapter

8

❖❖❖

Off the Beaten Track:
Heaven

"When you come to a fork in the road, take it!" This quirky quip is attributed to the sagacious baseball legend Yogi Berra. I have learned to view choices as an opportunity to reevaluate my plans. The most memorable incident of an unexpected fork presenting itself was when I was in high school, and I applied to become a short-term Rotary Exchange Student. I had never been out of the borders of South Africa, and I was enamored with the putative culture and history of Europe. After countless interviews and screenings, I was given my top pick of country to visit: Germany. I was overjoyed. We were informed that a young man from a tiny German town would be staying with us, and a few months later I would be staying with his family. Let's call him Hans.

I immediately began to learn some German so that I could assist Hans until he learned English. I diligently planned what local attractions I would take him to see and to which cultural festivals and experiences I would introduce him. We bought a second bed for my bedroom, cleared out half the shelves in my closet for his clothes, and purchased a school uniform for him so that he could blend in at my high school. Finally the day came for Hans to arrive. My parents reminded me that he would be tired after the flight and that I should not pepper him with questions about Germany and life in Europe. We waited for him at the airport toting a large welcome sign with the African motif. It was all very exciting. Until we met Hans.

My expectations, as it turned out, were out of sync with reality. Let's begin with the positive. Hans was fluent in English and quickly assured (instructed) me that I needn't try using the German I had attempted to master. Other than the facility of communication, there wasn't much else about our houseguest worth commending.

He came across as arrogant and antisocial and was unabashedly disinterested in our family or our culture. He refused to wear the school uniform, attended one day, and then announced he would not be accompanying me to school each day but would instead go sightseeing with his fellow exchange students from Germany. He lived out of his suitcase, which he kept locked, as if he didn't consider our shared room to be a safe place to store his belongings. And although he remarked how pleasantly surprised he was that South Africa had running water, he seldom bathed. His constant amazement that we possessed basic technology like television and refrigerators proved that he had done practically no research on our country.

You know that feeling when you realize your new car is a lemon? I felt rather shortchanged by this disappointment. The thought of living with him and his family in Germany suddenly lost its appeal. After Hans returned home, with only a week or so before I was scheduled to depart and join him, my parents and I contacted Rotary and asked them if there was a different family in Germany that could host me or, failing that, anyone anywhere in Europe who would take me in. The lady at Rotary explained sympathetically that Europe was the most coveted of their destinations, that all the slots for all the host homes had been filled, and that there was a waiting list of applicants wanting to go to Europe. But there was an alternative.

South Africa had very recently opened up an exchange program with Argentina, and there were ample families willing to host me there. That piece of news was completely unexpected. I had never contemplated visiting Argentina. Why would someone want to go to South America when they could go to Europe? No wonder they were desperate for applicants. Wasn't Argentina a Third World country? Did they have running water and refrigerators? All I knew about them was that they had a good soccer team and there was an Andrew Lloyd Webber song about crying for them.

I humbly admitted that my ignorance of the country was inexcusable, but I gambled that it couldn't be worse than sharing a room with Hans and his B.O. again. I agreed to be one of Rotary's guinea pigs. Since there had never been an exchange with South

America before, there was very little information about what to expect. And with scarcely any time to learn Spanish or research Argentina, I spent the days before my departure second-guessing my decision and hyperventilating when I thought of how dreadful the coming experience could be. But I had committed to take the road less traveled. And boy did it make all the difference!

My host family oozed with South American hospitality. They were friendly, unreserved, and passionate about everything. They fed me like a visiting king, and they lavished me with gifts. I was treated as a celebrity and was greeted by everyone I met as if I was a long-lost cousin. Being a teenager, I especially liked the cultural idiosyncrasy of being kissed on the cheek by every young lady I met. These people were nothing like Hans.

I have since visited Germany and met many warm, humble, and hygienic Germans. But I have never regretted switching my destination at the last minute. My only regret is that I didn't know how awesome the experience would be, so I could have anticipated it with more pleasure, rather than misplaced dread.

When studying any destination in depth, it behoves the diligent traveler to pause and reconsider his or her options, and ask, "Is there any alternate destination I should be exploring?"

We have looked in some morbid depth at Hell, but there is an alternative destination we should consider. With all that you know about Hell, you will admit that nowhere else could ever be as bad. But choosing Heaven as if it were only a desirable destination when compared to Hell is to miss the joy of anticipation for a superlative experience of breathtaking beauty and unsurpassed pleasure.

Here is a foretaste of glory divine—my personal recommendation to take the road less traveled, the narrow road to Heaven.

✢ BEEN THERE, DONE THAT ✢

Unlike Hell, the road to Heaven is not strictly a one-way street. There have been three credible people in history who have seen glimpses of Heaven and been allowed to talk about some of what they saw. In this chapter we will draw from what these eyewitnesses saw.

The Apostle Paul was granted the most privileged afterlife revelation of all, either bodily or in a vision. He said he was "caught up" to Heaven an experience that was so vivid that it was indistinguishable from a real-life visit.

✢✢✢

2 Corinthians 12: [2] I know a man in Christ who fourteen years ago was caught up to the third heaven—whether in the body or out of the body I do not know, God knows. [3] And I know that this man was caught up into paradise—whether in the body or out of the body I do not know, God knows—[4] and he heard things that cannot be told, which man may not utter.

✢✢✢

Regrettably, Paul was not permitted to tell of what he saw. So, no book deal and talk show appearances for the apostle.

Likewise, the people in the Bible who experienced resurrection, including Lazarus of Bethany, left no record of what they experienced.

Jesus obviously had a firsthand familiarity with Heaven. He, however, did not speak much about what Heaven was like. He was far more forthcoming about the nature of Hell. But Jesus did give hints about Heaven throughout his ministry.

The Apostle John was privy to the most detailed vision of

future prophecy, which he was uniquely permitted to describe in detail in his Book of Revelation.

Let's explore what we know about Heaven, drawing from the details in Jesus's parable of the rich man and Lazarus, his other teachings, and the vision John saw.

✣ HEAVEN IS A PLACE ✣

In the 1980s there was a popular song by Amy Grant in which she crooned, "Oooooh, heaven is a place on earth." According to the Bible, she was wrong. Just like Hell is a place, Heaven is a place too.

✣•✣•✣

Luke 16: [22] The poor man died and was carried by the angels to Abraham's side. The rich man also died and was buried, [23] and in Hades, being in torment, he lifted up his eyes and saw Abraham far off and Lazarus at his side.

✣•✣•✣

Although Heaven is in a different dimension than earth (to borrow Hawking's terminology again), it is in the same dimension as Hell. We know this because the rich man in Hell can see and communicate with Abraham in Heaven.

Some people think that Heaven is a bunch of puffy clouds with naked chubby cherubim playing harps. Or, alternately, that it is some sort of "state of being" or "level of consciousness." But according to the Bible, Heaven is a literal place. It is not a customized conglomeration of all the rewards your heart desires (*contrary* to the Robin Williams movie *What Dreams May Come*.)

Heaven is as literal as earth:

✣ Isaiah 66:1 says "Earth is His footstool, and Heaven is His throne."

✠ In John 14:2 Christ tells the disciples that "I go to prepare a place for you."

The way you get there is for your spirit to be absent with the body. Paul said "to be absent from the body is to be . . . present with the Lord." Since Jesus is in Heaven right now, seated at the right hand of God, that is where we go when we die.

The Bible describes Heaven's location as "up" and beyond the atmosphere, the stratosphere, and even the cosmos; or in Paul's terminology "the third heaven."

✠•✠•✠

1 Corinthians 12:[2-3] . . . caught up to the third heaven . . . into paradise—whether in the body or out of the body I do not know, God knows. . . .

✠•✠•✠

The real question on everyone's mind is, what is Heaven like, and what will we do there? Quite simply, Heaven is better, beautiful, and busy.

✠   HEAVEN IS BETTER   ✠

The most obvious aspect of the place Lazarus went when he died is that it's *better* than where the rich man went, and it's better than life on earth. You may agree that anywhere is better than Hell, but what makes Heaven so attractive is that it is better than earth.

Genesis 3 tells us that God cursed the earth in order to make mankind long for an eternity with him in a place that is better. If earth were fulfilling, no one would seek God. We were created to be in a relationship with our Creator, and he has hardwired us to feel unfulfilled until we are in a right relationship with him. Augustine said it this way: "We are restless until we find our rest in thee."

Heaven, on the other hand, is a place where there is no curse, and where everyone has been forgiven and made sinless (glorified). The people in Heaven are in a right relationship with God and with everyone else in Heaven.

✛ **1 Corinthians 2:** [9] But, as it is written, "What no eye has seen, nor ear heard, nor the heart of man imagined, what God has prepared for those who love him"—

✛ **2 Corinthians 4:** [17] For this light momentary affliction is preparing for us an eternal weight of glory beyond all comparison, [18] as we look not to the things that are seen but to the things that are unseen. For the things that are seen are transient, but the things that are unseen are eternal. [19] For we know that if the tent that is our earthly home is destroyed, we have a building from God, a house not made with hands, eternal in the heavens.

Paul is saying that Heaven is better, not merely better than Hell, nor simply better than earth, but better than anything anyone has ever imagined and better than anything else in the universe. Heaven is "beyond all comparison."

This superlative language still leaves large gaps in our understanding. If something is better than I can imagine, then is it futile to even try to picture it? Not at all. The Bible provides linguistic sketches to give us a framework with which to imagine what Heaven is like. Paul's only caution is that you not limit your idea of Heaven to what you are capable of conceiving in your finite mind. One area for which John provides copious detail is the physical appearance of Heaven's capital city, the New Jerusalem.

✛ HEAVEN IS BEAUTIFUL ✛

John supplies us with a breathtaking description of the central part of Heaven, a city called the New Jerusalem. The city is described as spacious, safe, and shining with light.

> Revelation 21: [10] And he carried me away in the Spirit to a great, high mountain, and showed me the holy city Jerusalem coming down out of heaven from God, [11] having the glory of God, its radiance like a most rare jewel, like a jasper, clear as crystal. [12] It had a great, high wall, with twelve gates, and at the gates twelve angels, and on the gates the names of the twelve tribes of the sons of Israel were inscribed—[13] on the east three gates, on the north three gates, on the south three gates, and on the west three gates. [14] And the wall of the city had twelve foundations, and on them were the twelve names of the twelve apostles of the Lamb. [15] And the one who spoke with me had a measuring rod of gold to measure the city and its gates and walls. [16] The city lies foursquare, its length the same as its width. And he measured the city with his rod, 12,000 stadia. Its length and width and height are equal. [17] He also measured its wall, 144 cubits by human measurement, which is also an angel's measurement.

Those measurements are probably a bit obscure to you, but a cubit is about 18 inches (45 cm), making the wall about 21 feet (6.5 m) wide (think Great Wall of China). A single stadion is about 607 feet (185 m), making the city's dimensions of 12,000 stadia the equivalent of a cube with length, height, and breadth of 1,380 miles (2,221 km). That's a city the size of Australia. And it has multiple levels in it, extending upward 1,380 miles.

This is a huge place. And that is just one city. Its gates are said to be perpetually open, and various denizens (angels and glorified, resurrected people) bring treasures into the city, presumably from their exploration of the universe (see Revelation 21:26).

The building materials in Heaven add to its luxury, radiance, and beauty:

Revelation 21: [18] The wall was built of jasper, while the city was pure gold, clear as glass. [19] The foundations of the wall of the city were adorned with every kind of jewel. The first was jasper, the second sapphire, the third agate, the fourth emerald, [20] the fifth onyx, the sixth carnelian, the seventh chrysolite, the eighth beryl, the ninth topaz, the tenth chrysoprase, the eleventh jacinth, the twelfth amethyst. [21] And the twelve gates were twelve pearls, each of the gates made of a single pearl, and the street of the city was pure gold, transparent as glass. [22] And I saw no temple in the city, for its temple is the Lord God the Almighty and the Lamb. [23] And the city has no need of sun or moon to shine on it, for the glory of God gives it light, and its lamp is the Lamb.

Cities of the ancient Near East were surrounded by walls. The wall in Heaven is massive and made, not of cheap brick, which needs to be painted, but a precious stone that possesses beautiful, luxurious color of its own. The rest of the city is constructed out of metal—gold, to be exact. A grade of gold we can't manufacture on earth. The more refined gold becomes, the lighter in color it becomes. Nine-carat gold is quite yellowish, but eighteen-carat gold is whitish with only a hint of pale yellow. Imagine 1,000-carat gold. It would be transparent, with only the hint of gold as light catches it. That is why John describes the city as clear as crystal. The city will look like it has been made of glass but without the fragility. There will be no cracks or smudges on its surfaces, which will also be shatterproof. It will be a glass like metal. How God gets it to be strong as well as beautiful is a mystery to me.

So, this is an enviable place to live. It sure beats the alternative. And it certainly beats your current hovel, no matter how luxurious you think it is. Imagine no litter, no degeneration, no rust or crumbling or cracks or mold or stains. Imagine no smoke or smog or pollution.

And all that is just the incidental location; it's the setting for everything else. A more astonishing attraction in Heaven is not the place, but the people.

✢✢✢✢

Revelation 21: [27] But nothing unclean will ever enter it, nor anyone who does what is detestable or false, but only those who are written in the Lamb's book of life.

✢✢✢✢

All the inhabitants are sinless beings who love and care for one another, are omni-competent, healthy, happy, and hard working. Every race and culture is represented there, and yet everyone is united in their beliefs, worldview, and mission. Everything revolves around pleasing God and others, not selfishness or survival.

Jesus called it "Paradise," which is reminiscent of the Garden of Eden, also called a Paradise. The Old Testament saints called it "Abraham's bosom," because being in Heaven was akin to being gathered to their fathers, emphasizing the fellowship and homecoming aspect of Heaven.

Heaven is literally glorious. It is saturated with the radiant manifestations of God's attributes. His goodness, beauty, power, wisdom, holiness, and majesty are all radiating from him and are clearly visible in all aspects of Heaven's design and construction and activity. Which brings us to another notable aspect of Heaven: it is busy.

⊹ HEAVEN IS BUSY ⊹

Satan has put some effort into making Heaven seem boring and unappealing. I once read of an English vicar asked by a colleague what he expected after death. He replied, "Well, if it comes to that I suppose I shall enter into eternal bliss. But I really wish you wouldn't bring up such depressing subjects."

The quirky cartoonist Gary Larson has one comic that portrays a lonely saint plopped on a cloud with nothing to do. The caption reads, "I wish I'd brought a magazine."

Randy Alcorn, author of the comprehensive theological work *Heaven*, writes,

⊹⊹⊹

I find it ironic that many people stereotype life in Heaven as an interminable church service. Apparently, church attendance has become synonymous with boredom. Yet meeting God—when it truly happens—will be far more exhilarating than a great meal, a poker game, hunting, gardening, mountain climbing, or watching the Super Bowl. . . . Will we always be engaged in worship? . . . if we have a broad view of worship, then the answer is yes.

⊹⊹⊹

The theologian, A. A. Hodge averred,

⊹⊹⊹

Heaven, as the eternal home of the divine man . . . must necessarily be thoroughly human in its structure,

⌑ 134 ⌑

conditions, and activities. Its joys and activities must all be rational, moral, emotional, voluntary and active. There must be the exercise of all the faculties, gratification of all the tastes, the development of all talent capacities, the realization of all ideals. Heaven will prove the consummate flower and fruit of the whole creation and of all the history of the universe.

✦✦✦✦✦

The Bible describes our activity as governing and our rewards as increased responsibility in God's every-expanding kingdom. René Pache described what we do as "centered more on activity and expansion, serving Christ and reigning with him . . ."

Alcorn shows from Scripture that Heaven may include an ever-expanding government, ongoing exploration of the universe, discovery of all the creatures, and plants and landscapes that God has created for us to find and enjoy and share and marvel over. I picture the place as *Star Trek* meets *The Chronicles of Narnia*. Imagine being able to try any activity you desire without the fear of being injured or killed. Imagine being really good at everything you try—mentally and physically—without the limitations you acquired on earth (like arthritis, a bad back, blindness, or a low IQ). And imagine it was all free. Heaven is not just better than Hell—it's better than anything or anywhere!

✦ THE BEST PART OF HEAVEN ✦

The most appealing part of Heaven as the Bible defines it is that Jesus himself will be there in all his glory. The New Jerusalem is like the capital city, complete with administrative headquarters for all of Creation and the King's personal residence. God's presence will be centrally located in the brilliance of glory and in the person of Jesus Christ.

✢ **Revelation 21:** ³ And I heard a loud voice from the throne saying, "Behold, the dwelling place of God is with man. He will dwell with them, and they will be his people, and God himself will be with them as their God. ⁴ He will wipe away every tear from their eyes, and death shall be no more, neither shall there be mourning, nor crying, nor pain anymore, for the former things have passed away."

✢ **Revelation 21:** ²² And I saw no temple in the city, for its temple is the Lord God the Almighty and the Lamb. ²³ And the city has no need of sun or moon to shine on it, for the glory of God gives it light, and its lamp is the Lamb.

✢ **Revelation 22:** ¹ Then the angel showed me the river of the water of life, bright as crystal, flowing from the throne of God and of the Lamb ² through the middle of the street of the city; also, on either side of the river, the tree of life with its twelve kinds of fruit, yielding its fruit each month. The leaves of the tree were for the healing of the nations. ³ No longer will there be anything accursed, but the throne of God and of the Lamb will be in it, and his servants will worship him.

The best part of Heaven is that we will see the face of the Lamb of God. You will see Jesus. And he will know you. And you will not be an enemy. There will be no need to be ashamed of your sin. You will be standing in his righteousness and reflecting his glory. The question is, is that what you want?

Pastor and author John Piper, in his book *God Is the Gospel*, poses this provocative question:

✢✢✢

If you could have heaven, with no sickness, and with all the friends you ever had on earth, and all the food you ever liked, and all the leisure activities you ever enjoyed, and all the natural beauty you ever saw, all the physical pleasures you ever tasted, and no human conflict or any natural disasters, could you be satisfied with heaven if Christ was not there?

❖❖❖

If you are not excited about being with Jesus forever, that is an indication that you do not yet know him in a saving way. There are people who want to be assured they will escape Hell, but they have no real desire to be in Heaven. They are like the ignorant crane in the old fable of the swan from Heaven:

❖❖❖

A Crane was scratching around in the mud looking for snails, when a Swan alighted next to him. He asked, "Where do you come from?" to which the Swan replied, "I come from Heaven."

The Swan then regaled the Crane with descriptions of the golden streets, pearly gates, sparkling rivers of life, and the incandescence of glory.

Eventually the Crane asked, "But are there any snails there?" "Snails?" asked the bemused Swan. "No."

To which the Crane replied, "It doesn't sound like I'd enjoy it much in Heaven."

❖❖❖

How about you? Does Heaven sound like a place you'd enjoy? There is no shame in admitting our internal GPS guidance system is faulty and that we've been heading in the wrong direction. Rather than continuing to explore the cul-de-sac of our own reasoning, perhaps it is time to trust God's map to Heaven, lest we end up surprised by Hell.

conclusion

❖ ❖ ❖

Unhappily Ever After

As the rich man looked across the chasm of regret that separated him from Lazarus, Abraham, and the Savior he had ignored, his thoughts turned to those yet living.

I called out "Then I beg you, father, to send him to my father's house—for I have five brothers—so that he may warn them, lest they also come into this place of torment." But Abraham's hands were apparently tied. I just could not bear the thought of my brothers also ending up here. If my fate could serve as a warning to others, I might find a modicum of solace in the knowledge my damnation was not in vain. But I supposes even that would be a mercy I don't deserve. The best I can hope for is that the living will somehow find, read, and believe the witness of Moses and the Prophets. If I knew then what I know now, I would invest every penny I had into caring for the suffering, giving them hope of their eternal comfort, proclaiming to them the gospel. And I'd buy them Bibles. Oh, would that every possession I owned could be sold to fund the publishing of the warning.

But, as part of my sentence, I will see more and more duped fools swept into this horrid place, minute by minute, day by day, for centuries. And every one of them staggers from the pain and heat, and stumbles in agony, only to look on what I have become and fear that their fate is now locked with mine. And then to see them catch the eye of those in Heaven, those we once knew, and mocked or ignored. It is too much for me. Oh for a moment of relief, for the bliss of sleep, for the distraction of a pleasure. But these thoughts of what I will never have are a whip I turn on myself.

My memory and my conscience burn me like hot tongs; a pain as bad as what my skin feels. The waves of repulsion I feel when I see the maggots squirm under my skin are as bad as the ripples of memories that lap at my conscience. I had so many chances to repent. I felt pangs of guilt so many times I could have acted on. I dismissed more beggars and worthy causes than I can count, and I ignored more pleas for mercy than I have uttered since my arrival here. I know I deserve this, and that is what makes it so damn hard to bear. I was surprised when I came, but now my being here makes more sense to me than the mercy I was granted in my lifetime. I did nothing to attract God's grace, but he poured it on me day by day. And now, what I wouldn't give for a drop of that goodness.

If anyone can hear me—listen. If anyone pities me—don't. You deserve what I am getting, but there is hope for the living: call on the Savior in the day when he can be found. Trust in him for salvation, and he will pay your debt for you, on the cross. And if you will not hear me, or Moses and the Prophets, or the testimony of the one who rose from the dead after three days in the grave, then may God have mercy on your soul . . . before it's too late. I don't mean to preach at you. But I do intend to strike fear in your heart. I wish you could come visit me for a moment—it would change your life, it would alter your eternity. To put it bluntly, it would scare the Hell out of you.

And now, as this misadventure comes to an end for you, it marks another beginning for me. Every day is as pointless as the day before, and no day gets me closer to escape or relief. And so I bid you farewell; for your sake I hope we never meet. Think on what you have learned. I shall simply go on and live unhappily ever after.

✦ ENDNOTES ✦

Introduction

10 "The Barna Research Group found": K. Connie Kang, "Next Stop, the Pearly Gates . . . or Hell?" *Los Angeles Times*, October 24, 2003.

13 "What many people don't know": Other writers in the New Testament, notably St. John's Book of Revelation, provide many details about Heaven (see Chapter 8), but Jesus himself never described the particulars of Heaven. However, in twelve passages, Jesus warned about Hell and often employed vivid terms; for example, he mentions unquenchable fire, torment, worms, and darkness.

Chapter 1

23 "A parable is a story illustrated": Sometimes Jesus used parables to explain truth; other times he used them to hide truth from those he didn't want to understand it (for example, Matthew 13:13).

26 "That historic sermon, preached on": From *Selected Sermons of Jonathan Edwards*, Gutenberg.org, accessed April 29, 2014, http://www.gutenberg.org/files/34632/34632-h/34632-h.htm.

28 "Here is another excerpt from the sermon": Ibid.

Chapter 2

34 "Others have done a fine job of that": See Alan E. Bernstein, *The Formation of Hell* (Ithaca, NY: Cornell University Press, 1993); Reverend F. X. Schouppe, *Hell: The Dogma of Hell, Illustrated by Facts Taken from Profane and Sacred History Plus How to Avoid Hell* (Rockford, IL: Tan Books, 1989); and Alice K. Turner, *The History of Hell* (New York: Harcourt, Brace, & Co., 1993).

34 "The Jews know it as": Robert Rainwater, "Sheol," in *Mercer Dictionary of the Bible*, ed. Watson E. Mills (Macon, GA: Mercer University Press, 1990).

35 "Islam's Koran (Qur'an) describes the place": Koran 101:9.

35 "Ancient Egyptians averred that those": Rosalie David, *Religion and Magic in Ancient Egypt* (New York: Penguin, 2002), 158–159.

35 "Mayans feared the nine-level realm": William Palmer III, "Maya Ballgame" (Orono, ME: University of Maine, Fogler Library).

35 "The Aztecs anticipated a frightening": M. E. Smith, *The Aztecs*, 2d ed. (Oxford, UK: Blackwell Publishing, 2009), 207.

35 "Celts called the haunted realm": "Uffern," in *A Dictionary of Celtic Mythology* (Oxford, UK: Oxford University Press, 2004).

35 "Slavs named the feared realm": William Shedden Ralston, *Songs of the Russian People* (London: Ellis and Green), 79.

35 "In ancient Asian religions, including": Anna L. Dallapiccola, "Naraka," in *Dictionary of Hindu Lore and Legend* (New York: Thames & Hudson, 2002).

36 "In the history of humanity": According to the *World Fact Book: Religions*, 2.01 percent of the world population in 2010 is atheist, though the number of people who are "non-religious" is higher. Those claiming to be Christians accounted for 33.39 percent. See https://www.cia.gov/library/publications/the-world-factbook /fields/2122.html#xx (accessed March 12, 2014).

Chapter 3

52 "These putative return-ticket holders": Bill Wiese's *23 Minutes in Hell*, or Mary Baxter (who claimed that Jesus accompanied her on a guided tour of Hell), for example.

56 "Some teach that when Jesus died": See, for example, Joyce Meyer, *The Most Important Decision You Will Ever Make* (Fenton, MO: Life in the Word, Inc., 1991), 35–37: "During that time He entered hell, where you and I deserved to go (legally) because of our sin. . . . He

paid the price there. . . . no plan was too extreme . . . Jesus paid on the cross and in hell." See also Frederick K. C. Price, *The Ever Increasing Faith Messenger,* newsletter, June 1980, 7: "Satan and all the demons of hell . . . dragged Him down to the very pit of hell to serve our sentence." Also see Kenneth Copeland, *Voice of Victory* (September 1991), 3: "He allowed Himself to come under Satan's control. . . . For three days in the belly of the earth, He suffered as if He'd sinned every sin that exists."

Chapter 4

62 "I'm not making this up.": Marge Floori, "Oil Drill Opens Hole into Hell," *Weekly World News*, October 2, 2008, http://weeklyworldnews. com/headlines/3060/oil-drill-opens-hole-into-hell/.

63 "Incidentally, previous infallible popes,": Pope John Paul II, public address to a General Audience, July 28, 1999, transcript located at http://www.vatican.va/holy_father/john_paul_ii/audiences/1999 /documents/hf_jp-ii_aud_28071999_en.html (accessed March 6, 2014). The quote is also found in Gustav Niebuhr, "Hell Is Getting a Makeover from Catholics; Jesuits Call It a Painful State but Not a Sulfurous Place," *New York Times,* September 18, 1999.

64 "On the other end": Rob Bell, *Love Wins* (New York: HarperCollins, 2011), 95.

64 "The Bible and many other religions": For example many religions have a tale of a descent in an afterlife realm. These include Osiris's descent in the ancient Egyptian *Book of the Dead* and Orpheus in Greek mythology. Gilgamesh in ancient Sumerian also descends to the underworld. In Mahayana Buddhism there is a tale of a descent into a hell-like nether region by Kuan Yin. And in Hinduism, Emperor Yudhisthira descends into Naraka.

64 "They don't call it the underworld": I've heard it said that some Eskimos believe Heaven is deep down in the earth, presumably because their

idea of utopia includes perpetual warmth. I haven't been able to verify that claim. But it makes for a quaint exception clause in the debate.

66 "Unlike Blake, Lewis believes that": As explained by C. S. Lewis's theological fantasy *The Great Divorce* (New York: HarperCollins, 2001, first published in 1946).

72 "That is to say, however": Scot McKnight, "Eternal Consequences of Eternal Consciousness?" in *Through No Fault of Their Own? The Fate of Those who Have Never Heard*, ed. William V. Crockett and James G. Sigountos (Grand Rapids, MI: Baker Books, 1991), 154.

Chapter 5

83 "For example, scholar John Gerstner": John Gerstner, *Repent or Perish* (Ligonier, PA: Soli Deo Glroia, 1990), 189–190.

84 "As scholar Robert Peterson explains": Robert A. Peterson, *Hell on Trial: The Case for Eternal Punishment* (Phillipsburg, NJ.: P&R Publishing, 1995), 187.

Chapter 6

102 "Here is an edited excerpt of": The interview aired on CNN's *Larry King Live,* on April 14, 2005, 9 p.m. Eastern Time. This excerpt is an edited version of a transcript I compiled from a video recording of the show. Emphasis added is mine. The official transcript is available at http://transcripts.cnn.com/TRANSCRIPTS/0504/14/lkl.01.html (accessed February 11, 2014).

Chapter 8

134 "He replied 'Well, if it comes to'": Barry Morrow, *Heaven Observed* (Colorado Springs, CO: NavPress, 2001), 89.

134 "Randy Alcorn, author": Randy Alcorn, *Heaven* (Wheaton, IL: Tyndale House, 2004), 188.

134 "The theologian A. A. Hodge averred": A. A. Hodge, *Evangelical Theology: A Course of Popular Lectures* (Edinburgh, UK: Banner of Truth, 1976), 399–402.

136 "Pastor and author John Piper": John Piper, *God Is the Gospel* (Wheaton, IL: Crossway Books, 2005), 15.

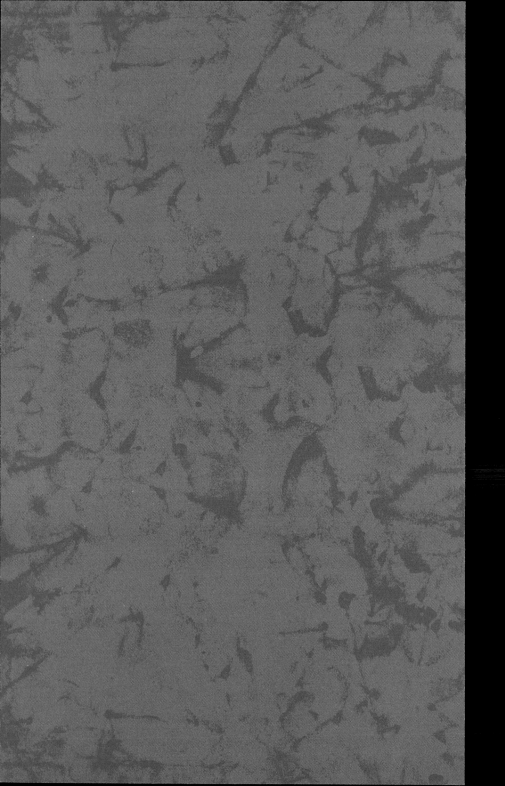

✢ RESOURCES ✢

Alcorn, Randy, *Heaven*, Carol Stream, IL: Tyndale House, 2006.

Bernstein, Alan B., *The Formation of Hell*, New York: Cornell UP, 1993.

Chan, Francis, *Erasing Hell*, Colorado Springs, CO: David C. Cook, 2011.

Craze, Richard, *Hell: An Illustrated History of the Netherworld*, Newburyport, MA: Conari, 1996.

Crockett, William V., and James G. Sigountos, eds., *Through No Fault of Their Own? The Fate of Those Who Hve Never Heard*, Grand Rapids, MI: Baker Books, 1991.

Edwards, Jonathan, *Sinners in the Hands of an Angry God and Other Puritan Sermons*, Mineola, NY: Dover, 2005.

Gerstner, John, *Repent or Perish*, Ligonier, PA: Soli Deo Gloria, 1990.

Hodge, A. A., *Evangelical Theology*, Carlisle, PA: Banner of Truth, 1976.

Konya, Alex, *Demons*, Schaumburg, IL: Regular Baptist Press, 1990.

Lewis, C. S., *The Great Divorce*, San Francisco: HarperOne, 2009.

MacArthur Jr., John F., *The Glory of Heaven*, Wheaton, IL: Crossway, 2013.

Meyer, Joyce, *The Most Important Decision You Will Ever Make*, Nashville, TN: FaithWords, 2003.

Morrow, Barry, *Heaven Observed*, Carol Stream, IL: Navpress, 2001.

Peterson, Robert A., *Hell on Trial: The Case for Eternal Punishment*, Phillipsburg, NJ: P & R Publishing, 1995.

Piper, John, *God Is the Gospel*, Wheaton, IL: Crossway, 2011.

Schouppe, F. X., *Hell: The Dogma of Hell, Illustrated by Facts Taken from Profane and Sacred History Plus How to Avoid Hell*, Rockford, IL: Tan Books and Publishers, 1989.

Turner, Alice K., *The History of Hell*, New York: Harcourt, 1993.

Audio Resources

Below are links to two sermons in audio form on the subject of Hell.

"The Agony of Hell," a sermon preached by Dr. Jack Hughes September 6, 2009, at Calvary Bible Church, Burbank, California: http://www .calvarybiblechurch.org/site/cpage.asp?sec_id=180007650&cpage_id =180020121&secure=&dlyear=0&dlcat=The+Gospel+of+Luke&ind ex=60 (accessed April 8, 2014).

"Surprised by Hell," a sermon preached by Dr. Clint Archer on July 14, 2013, at Hillcrest Baptist Church, South Africa: http:// baptistchurchhillcrest.com/sermons/?sermon_id=720 (accessed April 8, 2014).

"A Testimony of One Surprised to Be in Hell, Part 1: Luke 16:19 31," a sermon preached by Dr. John MacArthur on April 23, 2006, at Grace Community Church, Sun Valley, California: http://www.gty.org /resources/sermons/42-212/a-testimony-of-one-surprised-to-be-in- hell-part-1 (accessed April 8, 2014).

✦ ACKNOWLEDGMENTS ✦

This book owes its existence to the following faithful folks:

Patti Hummel
Kate Zimmermann
Keith Brown
Neil Swan
Hennie Vorster
Stan Webster
Mark Williamson
And my stunningly supportive wife, Kim.

❖ INDEX ❖

D

E

F

G

H

presence of Jesus, 135–137
separation from Hell, 53–54
Heaven (Alcorn), 134–135
Hebrews 10:29, 74
Hell. *See also* Eternity
  authority of God over, 83–85
  avoiding path to, 92–95, 113–114
  beliefs leading to assured entry,
    95–109
  descriptions, 12–14, 29, 55–56, 63–71,
    75, 87–89
  existence of, 10–15, 62–63
  levels of punishment, 73–75
  necessity for existence, 37–47
  no exit or second chances, 52–54,
    71–73, 78
  rationalizing safety from, 24–28
  religion and universality of, 34–37
  suffering of Jesus, 56–59
Hier, Marvin, 102–107
Hodge, A. A., 134–135
Hope
  Hell as absence of, 20–22, 52
  promise of salvation, 45–47, 141
  relying on false beliefs, 95–109

I

Inferno (Dante), 55, 69
Isaiah 14:9, 15, 65, 82–83
  14:9, 15, 65, 82–83
  55:6, 7, 97
  66:1, 128
Islam/Muslim, 13, 35, 103

J

Jahannam, Islamic concept of Hell, 35
James 1:17, 88
  1:17, 88
  2:10, 106
Jehovah's Witnesses, 42

Jesus
  acceptance as prophet, 13
  authority over demons, 57–59, 79
  authority over Hell, 85
  descriptions of Hell, 13–14, 143
  parable of master's return, 74
  parable of Lazarus and rich man,
    18–19, 87, 98–99, 128, 140–141
  parable of master's talents, 25
  parable of ten virgins, 25
  presence in Heaven, 135–137
  substitutionary rescue, 115–121
  suffering for sins of mankind,
    56–57
Jews/Judaism, 13, 34, 95–97, 103
Job
  1:6, 7, 81
  7:5, 10, 53–54
  17:16, 64
John
  5:25, 29, 85
  14:2, 129
  14:6, 7, 114
John Paul II (Pope), 64
Johnson, Ellen, 102–107
John the Baptist, 46, 96–97, 117
Judas Iscariot, 18, 74
Jude:6, 7, 57, 59, 69, 70, 72–73, 80

K

King, Larry, 101–107
1 Kings 8:46, 106
Koran (*Qur'an*), 35

L

Lake of fire, 68–70, 73, 80–82, 86
Larry King Live (TV interview), 101–107
Larson, Gary, 134
Law of Moses, 96
Lewis, C. S., 66

✦ ABOUT THE AUTHOR ✦

Dr. Clint Archer is a pastor of many years whose international ministry has taken him to twenty-two different countries so far. He has taught the Bible and preached in places as varied as Russia, Northern Ireland, Bhutan, and Egypt. He was raised in South Africa, lived on a kibbutz in Israel for six years, and went to school in the United States for six years before returning to South Africa to start a family and serve as senior pastor of Hillcrest Baptist Church in Durban, South Africa. He is a regular contributor to *Baptist Today* magazine and a weekly contributor to the TheCripplegate.com blog (readership 100,000). He regularly speaks at conferences related to biblical study such as the Rezolution Conference in Johannesburg and The Shepherd's Conference in California. He lives in South Africa.